Why Did You Say That?

Five Things Managers Say That Stifle Creativity

Bridget Tucker Smith

Copyright © 2024 by Bridget Tucker Smith

All rights reserved.

No portion of this book may be reproduced in any form without written permission from the publisher or author, except as permitted by U.S. copyright law.

Momma, Daddy, Mae-Mae, Michael, and Mark

Thank you for the love and the lessons.

YOU mattered.

Contents

Introduction	V
1. Leaders and Managers	1
2. Temper Your Passion	15
3. You Are Just ...	24
4. You Can't	32
5. It Is What It Is	43
6. This Is How We've Always Done It	51
7. Invest In You	73
8. Leaders And Managers Rewind	78
9. Inclusive Leadership	84
10. Communication Matters	98
11. Conclusion	113
Acknowledgements	117
Don't Quit Poem	121
Cross The Line Exercise	123
About the Author	127

Introduction

Why This Book Is For You

I've learned that I still have a lot to learn. I've learned that people will forget what you said, people will forget what you did, but people will never forget how you made them feel.

—Maya Angelou

Thank you for purchasing this book. It was written based on my experiences not only as a leader but also as a team member. Why Did You Say That? Five Things Managers Say That Stifle Creativity focuses on what managers convey to their team members, and how what they say can stifle creativity, halt productivity, cripple innovation, and sabotage growth. This applies not only to the person to whom the words are directed but ultimately, the team, the manager, the influence on the bottom line, and the return on investment for the entire company. It also applies to the employee who converses and ensures that what they say is said with the best intentions. Communication is important in building and guiding individuals, and it is critical that we never lose sight of how it can impact a career. The information contained herein will help you see all, or nothing: how words really matter when speaking with someone.

I chose the title Why Did you Say That? Five Things Managers Say That Stifle Creativity, based on some real-time sayings that have been said to me and I've witnessed being said to others. This book will share five sayings that I and others have heard managers say, along with some practical tips to enhance conversations. We will dive into how leaders and managers differ, and why it is important to truly understand how inclusive leadership and communication can be a foundation for excellence in empowering others as it serves as a catalyst for word choice when leading. Use my 'Invest In You' tips to help you have crucial conversations to spotlight details and aid you in reaching your potential by developing a growth mindset so that the words do not "get into your head" and interfere with your mission.

As a professional woman with 30+ years in the corporate sector, I have seen and heard a lot! I have worked at a top teaching hospital serving patients in the Critical Care space as a pulmonary function technologist, as well as a stint in the entertainment industry after the AIDS epidemic and serving in the biotechnology and pharmaceutical arenas. I have gone through extensive leadership programs, been certified in several business genres, and been led by some great leaders, a few who are now chief executive officers (CEOs) of some amazing companies! I have also been elected to chair organizations that stretched me and challenged my entire being. When the time came for me to lead a team, I reflected on those interactions - be they good or bad - to shape my leadership competencies to lead with intention, empathy, and purpose, while staying grounded with a strategic and growth mindset.

Those who don't read this book will keep feeling the sting of the tongue and not know how to handle miscommunications when they happen. They won't get the chance to hear how someone with extreme passion for their work has dealt with the negative words of managers and how these led to positive actions.

Grab a coffee or tea. Have fun, be engaged, and laugh a little. If this resonates with you, share it! We can change how we approach people one person at a time, one word at a time. We can lead better and in turn, make our organizations better. This book was designed for you to write in your reflections as you read along. You can also go to www.leadershiplanguagepractice.com and download the "free" accompanying workbook if you choose. Now, turn the page and let's get down to business.

Chapter 1
Leaders and Managers

> People ask the difference between a leader and a boss. The leader leads, and the boss drives.
>
> —Theodore Roosevelt

Before we tackle the five things that managers say that stifle creativity and halt productivity, I want to weigh in on the differences between leaders and managers. In my opinion, there is a difference. And words matter when spoken by both. Those differences can influence how one speaks and interacts with others, and how one is able to see the bigger picture in empowering others, while meeting people where they are and getting them to where they need to go. Grab your dictionary. How many of you still own one? As a noun, a leader is a person who guides or directs a group. An example of the ability to lead is the president of the United States. He has a vision to ensure that the US is dealing with its constituents and other governments with integrity. Whether you like him or not, his job is to maintain leadership of governmental bodies to influence positive outcomes for the country. Many people vote for words said and promises made. I try to look at what is being done and what needs to be done. Actions always speak louder than words. But, words can move mountains or crush valleys. Does the leader have the heart to bring people together? Can the leader respect the people whom they are leading? ALL the people?

Let's look at your chief executive officer (CEO), even if that's you. If you work for an organization or company, the CEO's job is to be the face of the company, and to have the strategic vision and foresight to put the right people in place to guide the company to profitability and sustainability. Being a leader, no matter the organization or team, brings with it an uncharacteristic ability to serve others while influencing behaviors to do the unthinkable. When one is chosen, elevated, tapped, pulled, made, or anointed into guiding others, the responsibility is filled with decisions as to how to impart wisdom and knowledge based on teachings and collected experiences. I have read many great books on leadership. A few of my favorites are as follows:

- *Leaders Eat Last: Why Some Teams Pull Together and Others Don't*, Simon Sinek, 2014, Portfolio/Penguin, New York.

- *The 21 Irrefutable Laws of Leadership: Follow Them and People Will Follow You*, John C. Maxwell, 1998, Thomas Nelson, Nashville, Tennessee.

- *Inclusion, Diversity, The New Workplace & The Will to Change*, Jennifer Brown, 2016, Publish Your Purpose Press, Hartford, Connecticut.

- *Leading Well From Within: A Neuroscience and Mindfulness-Based Framework for Conscious Leadership*, Daniel Friedland, MD, 2016, Super Smart Health Publishing, San Diego, California.

- *Whistling Vivaldi: How Stereotypes Affect Us And What We Can Do*, Claude M. Steele, 2010, W. W. Norton & Company, Inc., New York.

- *The Waymakers*, Tara Jaye Frank, 2022, Amplify Publishing, Herndon, Virginia.

All of these books help you to learn how to communicate as a leader, through your actions, words, and deeds. If you are not aware of your own biases, it's hard to lead and be fair to those who don't look, act, and think like you. All the above-mentioned books touch on the leader's ability to communicate and lay out a vision. Some people can't see right in front of them, let alone create a vision that spurs growth. Without a vision, there is no movement to bring dreams and plans to fruition. Without dreams and plans, there is no innovation and—without innovation—we lose value and stature as a respectful organization, and thereby stifle creativity.

During my attendance in a previous emerging leader development program, we took a course on crucial conversations. It was designed to teach us how to master tough conversations. Fast-forwarding to today, it was one of the best courses that I took during my time in the program, and I have used it on occasion with customers, teams, students, friends, family, and loved ones. It comes down to communication: Listening and asking poignant questions to gauge where people are so that you can serve them better. Conversing with intention hasn't always produced the outcomes I have hoped, but the mere fact that I have tried to better understand people helps me to meet them where they are as opposed to not engaging at all.

My undeniable definition of a leader is one who has the empathic skill of serving others when they can't see where they are going but who can help them attain the unthinkable because the leader cares. From my biblical studies, it reminds me of the shepherd who guides the sheep. The sheep don't know where they are going, but they have marked trust in their shepherd to lead them and keep them safe from predators. A leader guides with grace, transparency, and concern for their people in helping them to attain the best for themselves. The leader is part of the road map on one's journey to fulfilling one's passions, a cog in the wheel of destiny, bridging gaps and making dreams come true. It is not about the leader. When it is about them, and they exhibit signs of selfishness over selflessness, that's a red flag for me. It should be about you and the words they use to guide you. Good words can guide you to be great. Bad words can guide you to head out the door. Trust me on that—been there, done that! Leading commands attention to be intentional. It takes courage, empathy, and self-awareness to lead, as well as a little moxie and a whole lot of prayer. Word choice is critical when leading.

Think of your neighborhood boy scout or girl scout leader, your doctor, pastor of your church, your best friend, spouse, mom, dad, someone else who led you, and yes—even you. What did they do or say to you that enabled you to follow them? The proverbial, "Because I said so?" Ugh! I abhorred that statement as a child and vowed I would never use it as a parent. I DON'T. I want my daughter to know the "why" and have a conversation to understand the consequences that could arise from not doing the right thing. Stop and reflect on that for a moment.

Have you had a manager give you tasks to complete, or a leader coach and develop you to success? Check Yes_____ or No_____. They are both needed in organizations in some way. However, a leader moves their team in ways that everyone feels responsible for the outcome of that team or the organization. The culture starts with them and then everything that is done is built around that. What they say to you will speak volumes as to how you and your contributions are valued. If you checked "Yes," you are blessed to have been—or are being—nurtured by a person who understood their mission to serve as guardian of your heart, mind, and soul in the workplace, school, team, or organization in which you spend many of your waking hours. And you're probably enjoying mentoring and sharing with others. If you checked, "No," you are not alone.

Did you know that the average person spends 90,000 hours at work over a lifetime? That's 2,250 weeks and 43 years of working! And then, hopefully, you have some later years to enjoy life on your own terms and enjoy the fruits of your labor. Whew! That's a heck of a lot of work time in environments with folks who think differently, have differing values, and perhaps have not had the opportunity to work within a diverse team with a diverse group of people. You need to surround yourself with great leaders who lift you, communicate with you, and with whom you in turn can communicate. Everyone plays a part.

Think about something your best leader did to support you or teach you. What vision did they share for you or with you?

Write it here for reflection:

How did their care and compassion change your outlook?

Our father, Joe Tucker, was the leader of our family. At our house growing up, we didn't eat dinner until he came home so that we could have a collective conversation about our day. We talked about everything—from finances, church, sports to politics and careers. Daddy also had a vision of how he wanted his three children to move through the world and he began to speak about it as early as I can remember. Regardless of what negativity came, his positive words taught us how to overcome the negative and allowed us to design actionable steps to live purposeful lives. His positive reinforcements for forging an intellectual curiosity and thirst for knowledge were the hallmarks of our childhood. We were taught to never, ever, judge someone for whom they were, where they came from, how they looked, spoke, or how they moved through life. We were doing diversity, equity, and inclusion practices in our house before it even became a thing. It was a way of life in our house to include people. Now that I can look back on it with love and adoration, our father's daily talks on caring about others showed us through his army and civilian career, how he led his boy scout troop, and, being the patriarch of our family, that people came first if you were tasked to lead them. He is no longer here in the physical world, but his vision for our family and his words of encouragement have trickled down to me, my siblings, and our children.

We gained our entrepreneurial spirit from our mother, Ruth, and our grandmother, Lillie Mae. They had a way with words and could offer someone an opportunity without them realizing it or being forced to take it. Mom was our awesome girl scout leader, and our troop was always a top seller during cookie season. Mom could put something down on paper and turn it into reality. She started her own coat check business by having a conversation with a major developer in Atlanta to buy a company they were divesting in. Her courage and vision was critical to her start as an entrepreneur, but it was the way in which she lead that sparked passions in others, including her children.

One of my father's mantras that has always been top of mind for me throughout my life is Winston Churchill's "Never, never, never give up." It has been written that Sir Winston never said "Give up." My Dad added to that. In his speech to his alma mater, Sir Winston said:

This is the lesson: Never give in, never give in, never, never, never, never—in nothing, great or small, large, or petty—never give in except to convictions of honor and good sense. Never yield to force; never yield to the apparently overwhelming might of the enemy.

Basically: Never give up, stand firm in your beliefs, have conviction, don't back down. Words matter. I keep this mantra close to my heart during difficult times and even closer during awesome times. It is what I use when someone calls me "angry" because I ask a question to gain an understanding, or when microaggressions are directed at others and I stand in the gap for them due to misspoken words. My siblings and I are leading as our parents would have expected. It has not been easy dealing with the injustices that come our way, but we persevere in the face of them anyway. Those words mattered growing up and they still do. We carry them throughout our days as leaders of our own families, as well as the teams that we lead and have led. We have passed them on to our children. Mom and Dad would be proud.

What is a manager then? *The Merriam Webster Dictionary* says "A manager is a person who has control or direction of an institution, business, or a part, division, or phase of it including supervising and managing a group of people". They are supposed to lead. Many have a hard time. They focus on other tasks, which leaves no time for developing others. Managing tasks is easy: Leading is hard. Now, think of a manager who did or did not support or teach you? What did that feel like? Did they say anything to give you cause to pause?

Write your thoughts here:

Checking boxes is rote, sort of like math. Anyone can be a taskmaster. It takes a special person to manage tasks and lead at the same time. There are good managers and there are not so good managers. In my opinion, key differences involve the breadth and depth of experiences that one brings to the table when leading others. The varied experiences allow a person to insert themselves into another's shoes because they, too, have been there. It influences their word choice and inclusive nature. For instance, if a sales manager hasn't been at the bottom of the rankings, how in the world are they going to relate to that person who is at the bottom and trying to pull themselves up? How are they going to coach them forward? The "manager mindset" focuses so much on the data. The data is only half the story. It's not bad to focus on the tangible aspects of territory management, but what about knowing the person and their purpose? What gets people out of bed every day? For some, working is only about the bills, or the glamour of a position or title. And then there are those who care about the work that is being done to lead the team and accomplish huge feats.

When talking about this book as I was writing, many folks have had managers who didn't know much about who they were. You should know your people if you are tasked with leading them. This helps you to connect, understand each other's "why's", and build camaraderie. It helps you formulate conversations as you seek to learn about others. Connecting sends a human signal to another person that their value is not just tied to the bottom line. Your word choice will be intentional. Productivity is important, but people are more than the bottom line: the manager's mindset must readjust to move them to accomplish the objectives.

A few good books that I've read on the making of a manager that really give some good and practical tips on how to support teams and grow into a great manager are listed below:

- *We: How to increase Performance and Profits Through Full Engagement*, Rudy Karsan and Kevin Kruse, 2011, John Wiley & Sons, Inc., Hoboken, New Jersey.

- *Well Being—The Five Essential Elements*, Tom Rath and Jim Harter, 2010, Gallup Press, New York.

- *The First-Time Manager*—Loren B. Belker, Jim McCormick, and Gary S. Topchik, 2012, AMACOM, a division of American Management Association, New York.

- *First, Break All the Rules—What The World's Greatest Managers Do Differently*, From Gallup, 1999, 2016, Gallup Press, New York.

A manager can indeed be a leader. If purposeful, the roles converge every day. While the manager helps to accomplish a desired goal, their leadership kicks in as they authentically influence and inspire without the need to exert or exude power over others. A great manager leads and coaches their teams to excel beyond what they think they can do, monitors and directs their steps to get there, while providing avenues to bridge successes, support failures (we all have them), and amplify courageous leaps. A great manager chooses words to persuade versus dissuade.

Have you heard of the Peter Principle? Laurence J. Peter, in 1968, published a book on the hierarchical promotions of leaders. My take is this and I've seen it happen repeatedly. If a sales manager does well, they receive a promotion. This can also happen if they have a team that meets or exceeds numbers, deliverables, and expectations, which makes them look good, yet the manager doesn't serve as a good leader. As one would expect: The data shows team success and is used to justify the promotion, but it could be the employees' drive and incentives to perform—not anything the manager has done. The data shows that they are doing well in that role and they get promoted again. This cycle continues until they reach a point where they are at a position that is desired. Many of us have seen this cycle occur in our organizations. What is usually amiss is the leadership training that managers need to guide and influence their teams, both collectively and individually. Some take the initiative to gain experience; others don't. The ones who don't are ill-equipped to lead teams to greatness. They become mediocre at best, and their team becomes lackluster in its performance because there is no effective leader, unless there is another one leading from their seat to support the growth of the team.

To validate their thoughts, Allen Bensen of the University of Minnesota, Danielle Li of MIT, and Kelly Shue of Yale, analyzed the performance of 53,035 sales employees at 214 American companies from 2005 to 2011. In that time frame, 1,531 of the sales reps were promoted to become sales managers. The data was able to show that the best salespeople were more likely to be promoted, yet also to perform poorly as managers. Why do you think that is? From experience, many of us know that the top-performing people don't always make the best managers. Many of you have seen countless times that those are the people who get promoted. The skills needed are different, and a person does not always transfer to being a great leader because managing oneself is much easier than managing others. The relevant skills are not acquired by the ability to decipher data: They are built by gaining an empathic understanding of what motivates your people, and how to keep them engaged to reach their professional goals and the goals of the company. It takes self-awareness and compassion. If those two characteristics exist, it's a start to having meaningful conversations, garnering respect for others, and ensuring that the words you use are helpful and not harmful. The people who quickly become involved in managing others roll up their sleeves, collaborate without judgment, understand that inclusion is a strength not a weakness, and lead with empathy and integrity—they are the ones who move mountains. They are visionaries and often have a strong passion for doing the job.

The introspection, feedback, and reflection that has helped me to be the person and leader that I am today has also enabled me to motivate people up, down, and sideways. Trust me on this: I have made mistakes and am harder on myself than anyone. Self-reflection continues to teach and humble me every single day. The one thing I want you to remember is that you are valuable as you are, no matter what anyone says about you— or *to* you. Your value is not attributed to anyone's opinion of you, or the words that they use to sway you. Words matter. Nowadays, when someone is promoted, there isn't enough time and money spent on training to build their existing skills or develop any potential ones. It is very disappointing: The person promoted usually doesn't get a fair start and the team they are to lead suffers due to insufficient training. Careless mistakes inevitably occur, which ultimately affects both trust and the bottom line. Leadership development is critically important and empowering, and it should be mandatory for all new leaders regardless of successful sales execution. An effective leader will strive to understand their team, be transparent in their communication and delivery, and—ultimately—lead with intention.

Now that we've discussed the differences between leaders and managers, let's talk about the five sayings that can affect how a manager leads and how what they say can derail a team, impact productivity and innovation of those they are assigned to lead, and diminish trust. The end result is people leaving to find better leaders to collaborate with and learn from. Don't be dishonest with the people you engage with. Show up in truth. You'll be free to be your authentic self and find joy in what you do, regardless of what anyone says to try and discredit you, belittle you, admonish you, and/or stifle your creativity. Words matter. Choose yours wisely.

In the next chapter, we will discuss one of the 1st things people say that can stifle your creativity and halt productivity. Sit back, and ask yourself some questions as you read. This happened to me so I will meet you where I've been. Let's go! 'Temper Your Passion'. Nah!

Chapter 2
Temper Your Passion

A burning passion coupled with absolute detachment is the key to all success.
—Mahatma Gandhi

Words can be helpful or hurtful. We know that. Has a manager or former manager ever said something so crazy that you looked in utter amazement and said in your head, "What did they say?" Better yet, "Why did they say that?" Did they crush your spirit or say something that gnawed at your confidence? Please raise your hand, nod your head, or roll your eyes. I am rolling my eyes as I write this. I feel you. It has happened to me and I have seen it happen to others several times—too many times to count.

Those who truly know me know that I am very passionate about the people, things, and causes that I care about. And I will admit it. There are times when I am overly passionate about something and will not back down on what I think is fair, appropriate, and right for whatever is being pursued. Suppose you are in a team and have been very successful not only in your role but also in helping to elevate your entire team and organization. You've managed to become highly adept at navigating your workplace environment, community, and the constituents whom you serve. What motivates you is the work that you do. It's what gets you out of bed every single day. Imagine being told to 'Temper Your Passion' when you are bold enough to ask questions for understanding and giving suggestions to improve an outcome. Had I been wearing pearls, I would have clutched them in sheer dismay at being shocked by such a statement! Excuse me? What does that even mean? In my mind, I heard, "Be quiet." *Why did they say that?* What was said was "Don't speak with so much enthusiasm." "Not everyone exhibits your level of passion." "No, not everyone exhibits my level of passion. What irks me is that people don't seem to care about others. I try to advocate for those who can't advocate for themselves."

We have differing degrees of passion, but I should not have been singled out because my degree of caring was different. What was the real issue? I came to do a job that spoke to my heart. I replied that I couldn't temper my passion because it is what drives me. It is what fuels my desire to be better and to make the world a better place. It is how we serve others who need advocacy. If people don't have passion, they don't have purpose. It made me feel unheard and—quite honestly—invisible, and annoyed. Not long after that, a young woman was hired to join the same team, and the first thing that was said about her was that she was what? Passionate. Eye roll. That day,

I decided that I didn't know whether I could work in an environment like that.

As I sat in the quiet of my room, I thought about it and wanted to better understand what was meant by that statement. What I felt was not making me feel too good because it suggested to me that my concern for what we were trying to accomplish was being taken for granted and that I was being silenced. I understand that not everyone is as passionate about what they do, but to tell someone that is insensitive. I needed to better understand and examine what I say, so that my statements aren't misconstrued and no one thinks I am angry. There is a whole lot to be angry about but, for me, I'd rather put my energies into making things better for all.

What I have learned throughout my career and motherhood is that words really do matter. Words can sting or they can charm. If used inappropriately, they can shut people down, and that affects how and when things get done. Nothing gets done when people are misunderstood, hurt, aggravated, and devalued. Sometimes the lack of words sends signals too! Silence can be a strong predictor of buy-in or not. There are times when you may have to elicit a strong response to a person who isn't quite cutting it, but there is a way to say it. When the tongue stings, it can "twist your wig" as my grandmother used to say!

I have been passionate about all my roles, and my intentions for working in the field I am in comes from having been a patient and advocating for patients. Some time ago, I spoke out loud about an injustice. I didn't curse at anyone. I didn't curse anyone out. I was upset about how something was handled. I was reprimanded. For months, I was iced and siloed from my team, listening to others cursing while I remained quiet. I learned the hard way when talking, even about oneself. I should be careful in speaking my mind to lessen any embarrassment. I checked myself, accepted responsibility, and apologized for my mistake. When asked why it had happened, I was told that it was done to "put me in my place." Okay, so now I wanted to curse, but I kept quiet. Excuse me. Oh no, I couldn't believe what I heard. Exasperated, I had to grin and bear it. I vowed to not let my past define my future and to keep it moving. The dialogue between two people can bring about an understanding to encourage effective communication. When words are used intentionally, to understand and not harm, this builds respect, and can clarify any misunderstandings.

How did I move forward and what can **you** do to shift your mindset when something like this happens? Yes, you're going to want to roll your eyes. Don't do it. Think before you speak or keep your mouth shut. 'Invest In You.' What do I mean? Here is what I did to help me move into shifting the narrative for me and keeping it positive, while propelling forward.

'Invest In You.' When no one else will, ensure that you take the necessary time to reflect on what happened, determine how you can adjust, and still feel as though you are doing the work that you have been preparing to do.

I*Initiate a conversation to understand the context of a response and clarify your statement.

N*Nurture your inner ability to grow and succeed. Collaborate with those who can help you.

V*Value who you are. No one's perception of you determines your trajectory. Keep telling yourself that.

E*Empower yourself to hone your skills (i.e., get a certification, enroll in a course).

S*Seek a coach to traverse the journey with you. Leadership coaches are great. There are many to choose from. I have a good one.

T*Trust your gut. Always.

In both cases, I had a brief conversation to understand where there was, if any, a misstep on my part. After introspection, I noted that my passion IS what guides me. I cannot, and do not, expect others to have the same level of passion as me. I learned so much on both of those days, some eight years apart. I also know that people make mistakes, managers included, and they should own up to the mistakes when made. Trust is hard. What I do expect is that people should listen to what is being said, not take it personally, not quote what is being said out of context, and think before they elicit any responses that could damage the trust.

If you are going to lead a team, it behooves you to really understand your team members and what motivates them. Perhaps mentioning that: "You know, you're very passionate and it shows in how you love what you do. People have different reasons for why they do what they do. When you are conversing, try to be mindful that not everyone is here for the same reasons as you are." That would have been better received than 'Temper Your Passion.' Try to make things better from your seat. Oftentimes it takes courage to be authentic, even when you feel you cannot be. I believe that most people want to love their jobs. Since we spend most of our lifetime working, we should really like what we do. It helps when you have a leader that can see through the madness, and decipher the intent.

Knowing your team, and their "why", helps you as the leader to guide people to destinations they never dreamed of. If you can humble yourself and step into someone else's shoes, you'll learn a little bit about them and a lot about you. Your conversations will be intentional and your word choice will propel people to move mountains. It is worth the ride to self-discovery.

What would you have done if this happened to you?

If you are a manager or team member, before you address anyone: **STOP** before you say anything, **THINK** and ask questions.

<u>**Treat** others as you would like to be treated</u>.

How would you like it if one of the people you led acted in a not so cool way to you? Even if you feel that someone is more tenured, accomplished, or better looking than you, there is never a time to be rude and demeaning. The golden rule is the golden rule for a reason. It makes sense and is practical when collaborating and working in teams to get things done for the group that you work with and the organization that you work for. Ask if there is something you can do to make things better. You set the tone as the leader and should never buy into the drama that can exist within a team. If you're the one leading the drama, that's another problem.

Hone your skills as a leader.

Take some classes; enlist the services of a mentor. If you have never been a manager, read a few books (see the list in Chapter 1), or join a development program. It could help to have someone you can rely on to give candid feedback. After all, thoughtful feedback is indeed a gift. It's free advice that you can take or leave. It's up to you.

Lastly, invest in the services of a leadership coach. There are plenty around these days and they are eager to support individuals who cannot move their leadership abilities forward.

Influence your followers by engaging authentically.

Be authentic yourself. If you are truly a leader, your first inclination is to serve others outside of yourself. You are a servant leader. You work for the team that you are assigned to lead and the people whom you encounter. The best leaders are those who, when they make mistakes, own up to them, look for ways to pivot, ask for feedback, thank those who provided feedback, and move forward in developing as people. People like working for people like that. It helps teams to be more authentic and feel connected. There is nothing wrong with being your true self. There are ways to say things positively to encourage others to develop. That's your job as a leader.

Never belittle anyone.

There are times when someone is going to be better than you, but at no time should you, the manager, ever belittle anyone. The best leaders have spheres of influence that they can tap into when needed when mistakes are made, or they want to be better. If you are a parent, would you belittle your child? If so, you're not nice. Get help.

Know your biases.

This is critical as a leader. Understanding your biases will aid you in making decisions that can affect your entire team either negatively or positively. Your job is ensuring that the people who you are tasked to lead feel included and safe in their skins. They should feel that they are visible, and that their opinions and experiences matter. If you don't know your biases, get help in doing so. At the time of this writing, there are many courses available and so many people waiting to help you discover how and where you can shift and develop. Take a course on LinkedIn such as 'Diversity Inclusion with Empathy' by Sharon Steed. Doing so can help strengthen your team and your interactions with others.

Give appropriate feedback. What is important is that you are transparent in how you approach the people whom you are tasked to lead. Your authenticity as a leader drills down to your team being authentic with you, thereby building a trusting environment in which everyone thrives and reaches their goals for you, the team, and the company or organization that you work within.

In the next chapter, we will explore the 2nd saying that can make you feel small, but I'll help you to rise above it and stand tall. You are always better than 'You Are Just ...' You are simply "You" and you are valued. Words really do matter.

Chapter 3
You Are Just ...

What matters most is you have been given life. Make the most of your existence.

—Lailah Gifty Akita

You. *Who are you?* Are you someone's mother, father, brother, sister, wife, husband, cousin, aunt, nephew, uncle, friend? You get it. Right now, I want you to pick up your phone, smile, and take a picture. Look at it and say, I am a bada**! If you can honestly repeat that daily, it will help to build up an internal firewall that will not allow the things that people can say to you hurt you. Oh, it may sting, but you will be able to handle the negative and turn it into a positive. You won't crumble like a cookie. But, if you do momentarily, you won't stay crumbled for long.

You were created to be here at this very moment in time. You have a purpose, and I am truly a firm believer that no one can stand in the way of what is for YOU. Oh, we know how hard folks can try to obstruct your path. But I do know that, if the path is illuminated and heavenly designed with intention, stay on it and—as my father once told me— "Let nothing or nobody rain on your parade!" I look at that saying every single day, and it moves me and keeps me focused.

Has anyone ever said, 'You are just a ...' when they are telling you about yourself? 'You are just a mom, You are just a dad, You are just a friend, You are just a husband, yada yada, yada.' You know there is a story to this. Sit back and read this one:

In a previous company where there was an open-door policy to engage with senior leadership, I did exactly that to seek information about a position that was to report to the senior leader. I sent an email to put time on the calendar to discuss an option that I wanted to have them weigh in on. Matter of fact, it was about an opening that I felt I wanted to apply for, because I had been doing the job already and wanted to ask the hiring manager about it. I also let the interim manager know and was told, 'You can't do that, you are just an account manager.' What do you mean, I am just an account manager? I am not just anything." I had been holding the team down in ways that were advantageous for the group. My daughter is not just my daughter and I am not just her mother. Jesus is not just Jesus. JESUS IS JESUS! OMG! What were they trying to say? Whatever it was, it was not resonating with me.

Let's break this conversation down into smaller chunks so that, if anyone ever says something as mundane and outrageous to you, you will be able to handle it with laser-like precision and keep it moving. What does "just" mean? According to *Merriam-Webster*, "just" can be used as an adjective or an adverb. As an **adjective**, it can be used as a **reasonable** synonym for having a basis in, or conforming to, fact or reason. In a sentence, you might say, 'She had just reason to believe she was in grave danger.'

If "just" is used to conform to standards of correctness, with "proper" being the synonym, the sentence could go something like, 'We are serving just proportions', meaning calculated sizes. Another example is "just" being what is "merited" or "deserved" as the synonym: 'He received a just punishment for the convicted crime.'

As an **adverb**, "just" takes on a different meaning: 'The measurements were just right,' meaning exact and precise. For time meaning, think of 'the school bell just rang': Time to change classes or leave for the day. Think of your favorite sports team and watching a game: 'The punter missed the field goal by a very small margin. It was just too late.' 'Just be yourself' means simply being you. When you say, 'This is just wonderful,' it means something is very cool, amazing, and awesome. And, lastly, 'When it just might work' means it is possible.

When you say to someone 'You are just a worker, teacher, account manager, etc.', it has a negative connotation. You are minimizing their possible existence as a person in their chosen occupation. When that was said to me, I felt small. What it really implied, whether said or not, was that my title of an account manager did not warrant the time that I had scheduled with the VP or the ability for me to even inquire about the role. It felt as though I was being made to feel 'less than,' especially given the tone in which the words were spoken. It was downright mean and it was not cool. It was demoralizing and I certainly did not want to work with that person or anyone like them. I was once told that I didn't want to have the title that I had. It wasn't that: I wanted to do the work that I came to do yet was unable to do. My expertise and passions were not being utilized. I already know that I am more than a title. Titles don't make people: People make people. You are more than a title.

Because someone has a title does not give them carte blanche to act rudely and say demeaning things to the people they lead. It is quite the opposite if one is leading teams. There are managers that lead teams that do not have the bandwidth, lack emotional intelligence and empathy as well as the competencies to lead. Some companies have great leadership development programs for FIRST TIME managers, others do not. People look for answers from people they trust. Sometimes a manager isn't trustworthy because it is all about them and they can't seem to get out of their own way. Ever been on a team like that?

How did I work through this one? It was a tough one. Indeed, I had to ground myself in prayer and solicit the help of a mentor. I think everyone should not only have a mentor but a great life coach on speed dial. All of them have helped me tremendously as I have navigated these leadership waters. So, what did I do?

I*Initiated a conversation to better understand where the manager was coming from and what they meant. Had a conversation with another person to walk through this scenario and receive secondary feedback.

N*Nurtured my inner ability to grow and succeed by going on to have a meaningful interaction with the VP to gauge what they were looking for. Collaborated with those who could support me and decided to pass on employment there.

V*Valued myself by investing in my sanity and mental health. Again, no one's perception of you determines your trajectory. Keep telling yourself that. Don't surround yourself with people who make you feel small with their words. Be around people who lift you up and support your development so that you can be a champion for others.

E*Empowered myself and found a new job. Hone your skills (i.e., get a certification, enroll in a course).

S*Sought a coach to traverse the journey with me. Enlist the support of a leadership coach to talk through scenarios and prepare you for what is to come next. Mine was amazing.

T*Trusted my gut. Always. I trusted my gut and walked away. This warrants repeating: Trust your gut. Always.

What could have made this scenario better? To be honest, after being asked about it, one way would have been for them to apologize. Secondly, it could have been said that the manager wanted me to go through them, instead of directly to the VP. That was done after it happened and the words already spoken. We had an open-door policy. Why do we tell people to do one thing when we want them to do something else? Organizations should not create mundane policies for the sheer benefit of doing so. Policies need to be revised and scaled for different outcomes. This encounter was mean-spirited. Ultimately, the manager decided not to lead a team anymore and I decided to leave because the behavior was tolerated with no accountability.

What would you have done if this had happened to you?

If you are a manager or team member, before you address anyone: ***STOP*** before you say anything, ***THINK*** and ask questions**.**

Be **tactful.**

You can say what you need to say to someone, but there is always a way to say it. If you need to discipline a person, you can have a conversation, by first reading the room to ensure that they are ready to receive your message. Discipline them quietly, not in front of team members. Don't do that. You never know what is going on with someone until you ask. Choose your words smartly.

Practice **humility**.

Are you right? Is what you saw or heard for real? Could you have been wrong? Could someone else have been wrong? Could they have miscalculated what had happened? Humble yourself and ask clarifying questions so that you can determine whether you are right. Passing judgment could be detrimental if you are wrong. Humble yourself before you make a grave error that can potentially harm a person's character. People can lie to get others in trouble without understanding the nuances of a situation.

Focus on **inspiring**.

Leaders inspire. Managers task. Be a leader. Your job as a leader is to empower and uplift your direct reports, teams, and anyone who is in your sphere of influence. Who wants to work for—or with—someone who lacks emotional intelligence and empathy? Without those, you can't put yourself in someone else's shoes to guide them to unimaginable heights.

Be **Nimble**.

You must be quick on your feet. This reminds me of a fast running back in football. With his speed, he can change direction in the blink of an eye. Be ready to pivot. Read the room.

Knowledge is power.

Always keep learning. Leaders never stop learning how to lead. Read a book (see Chapter 1). Speak with a friend. 360 feedback can give valuable insights. Don't be afraid to use the gift of feedback when given and used in the right way. It is meant to help you develop.

In the next chapter, we discuss the 3rd saying that is annoying. You can do anything that you attempt to do. You may not be able to do it today, but tomorrow holds promise. Some things can wait, but don't let 'You Can't' stop you from dreaming and being you. You are a gift of value.

Chapter 4
You Can't

You have to find what sparks a light in you so that you in your own way can illuminate the world.

—Oprah Winfrey

You should not say, 'You Can't.' Why? Because saying 'You Can't' without an explanation as to why doesn't help others understand what you mean. It's a one-sided conversation. But then, I don't think saying "You can" is good either: It depends on the situation, what you're doing and when you're doing it. Case in point: When I was a kid and it was raining outside, I heard my parents say, "You can't go outside." Me: "Why? Okay, I understand that it is raining, but what if I wanted to get wet and play anyway?" They weren't worried about the rain. It was the lightning storms. By explaining their reason for not allowing me to do that, it made sense, even as a kid. Who wants to get struck by lightning? Sometimes we got caught in the rain walking home from school or playing a game in the rain. It was so fun. What was the difference? When my daughter was young, she loved going out in the rain. I didn't tell her she couldn't go out—I armed her with an umbrella, coat, and boots to stomp in the puddles. It was a lesson in **You Can't** do this, but **You Can** do this. It brought her sheer joy.

The dictionary doesn't define 'You Can't' and we are going to have to look at this in terms of when it is appropriate and when it is not. To tell someone they can't drive down a mountain at 100 mph is one thing. Who wants to do that? Who has time to explain everything said to every person? Or to tell your kid they can't have peanuts because they are allergic is another. I can't eat shellfish. I am allergic. No crab, no lobster, no catfish (because they eat shrimp), etc. I can't eat walnuts because I am allergic. I do not want to look like a puffer fish, with watery eyes, and my throat tingling and itching. Therefore, I don't eat walnuts or shellfish because I can't. Simple as that.

How did it feel when someone told you that you couldn't do something that you wanted to do? Did you take responsibility to inquire for yourself as to why you couldn't do what you wanted to? Write it here.

When you're told that you can't do something, it sparks a question. Why can't I? There are many answers and the onus is on you to have a conversation to find them out. Is it because you don't want me to? Are you questioning my ability? Is it not a good idea? The best answer is always going to be a reasonable explanation of why not. Not, 'Because I said so,' or 'It Is What It Is.' I do not like that statement at all. It is true in some respects, but it still drives me crazy (see Chapter 5).

Words matter so much when trying to convey excitement, disappointment, encouragement, and when having meaningful conversations. In this business that I am in, I have been told countless times that I can't lead a team because I haven't led a team before. Well, that is not true. I have not led a team in the way in which the industry that I work in categorizes its managerial roles. We need to change that. I have led several successful teams and coached my team members to new roles, new heights, and affected the bottom line positively while doing so, and empowering them to dream big and go after what they need for themselves and their families. Isn't that what leadership is about? I really like your background, but I can't hire you. But you can hire that other person with no experience, no record of leading teams, volunteer or paid? Really?

The Peter Principle takes full effect here. We talked about it in Chapter 1. A sales rep does a great job selling, achieving their quota, moving the business. Their manager moves them to the next role; no experience leading any kind of team; no leadership development training (it's one thing to sit through a simulation versus actually leading and coaching others in real time); friends hiring friends and unable to understand how their leadership (or lack thereof) will impact the trajectory of others. Sheer numbers and expectations that one will be a great leader are seemingly what matter. I believe great leaders don't always have stellar numbers. What great leaders possess is the grit to persevere and the grind to get out of the pit. They are visionaries and can see around the corner and anticipate ambiguous challenges. They also recognize that they can pull others up by sharing their successes and failures. They can be proud of those who soar past them because—guess what?—it isn't about them. For the most part, great leaders try to see the very best in people and meet them where they are. At least, that is what I've learned. And any identified weaknesses can be viewed as underwhelmed strengths that make for great leadership development stories. It is what makes their word choices matter when speaking with you.

When a person is told they can't do something without explanation or in an abrasive tone, it signals that they whom you have deemed to trust either isn't self-aware of how they can assist you or there could be feelings of intimidation or inadequacy on the manager's part whereby they don't want to help you. In a hierarchical organization, and I've seen it happen, where many managers have been the least trained, yet they are tasked with the major day-to day duties of running a team to empower people to be their very best and improve business outcomes. They could not move the team forward.

Knowing what I know now about building financial literacy, I was able to guide my daughter as she was making some key decisions for college and life after college. As she was telling me what she wanted to do and be in life, I didn't say, 'You can't be this or that.' I told her she could do anything she put her mind to and put the work in to get there. Now that she is grown, my conversations are more centered around the following: make sure, whatever you do, you can sustain yourself. Building wealth creates freedom. The freedom to choose what you want to do on vacation, where you live, etc. Based on your dreams and aspirations of how you want to interact with the world, choose wisely. Preparation is key and communicating what you need to get there is paramount. My dad would be proud of that conversation.

Here is another scenario that can happen. Say an employee wants to take a vacation and is told that they can't. No other reason is given other than 'You Can't.' Is there an underlying reason as to why they cannot take their vacation time? Did they give the proper notice if warranted? Vacation time is personal time off. If there is a reason as to why you are not able to take the vacation, you should know that reason and the person denying it should be prepared to explain and collaborate on suggestions to address your absence. If you must change your plans due to reasons that your absence would cripple the team and/or a project, then perhaps rescheduling or finding alternative dates would be helpful. But telling someone they can't take their vacation time isn't cool, especially if there is no policy to denote the how to's. Adaptability is a key leadership characteristic that is important. There could be a myriad of reasons why the answer is 'no', but it helps the person to understand why when there is.

Let's say that workflow adjustments may be impaired due to someone taking time off. Why not have someone cover for the person so that they can take their vacation? The business still gets done. There have been times when several people on previous teams have covered for one another. It was extremely helpful and, for the person taking the vacation, it afforded some comfort knowing that one of your teammates was prepared to support you while you were out. It also let your customers know that you cared about business being conducted in your absence. Perhaps the person can put in extra hours before their leave to ensure that their area has additional coverage and expectations are set for what business gets done while they are gone. In our business, we can work longer days to make sure that we have reached everyone we need to converse with before we leave for some downtime. Not every company has thousands of employees. Some companies have 10, 20, 50, 100 … employees. It is important to be willing to have critical conversations in order to understand what needs to occur to keep the business running. Those business rules and words matter for any size business.

When I think of how 'You Can't' can totally belittle someone in the workplace, I remember the shameful 'You can't sit with us' quote in *Mean Girls*, which was a very popular movie back in 2004. Did you see it? It is a lesson in diversity, equity, inclusion, and belonging. The gist of the scene is the rich girls ('mean girls' in the movie), with an elitist attitude, did not want one of their friends to sit with them at lunch because she was wearing sweatpants!

They were always dressing up and they made her feel uncomfortable. Get the movie! There are a lot of lessons on belonging and inclusion in it. We will talk a little about that in Chapter 9 on Inclusive Leadership. I will not spoil the movie for you but pay attention to what happens when the choice of words is used throughout. It is a lesson in humility. Words matter. 'You can sit with us' sounds great, feels so much better, and is inclusive. You feel seen. You feel welcomed. You feel like you matter. You do matter. Sweatpants are amazing! Wear them.

So how do we get past this 'You Can't' saying and look at how it can be used for good positive intentionality. I like to think of 'You Can't' as 'You cannot at this time' or 'You cannot do it this way, but let's look at alternative ways to accomplish your objective.' Specifically in the workplace, there are times when it isn't the right time for many reasons. You haven't honed and sharpened the right skills yet. You work for someone who doesn't see your value. Can I get a witness? Raise your hand.

You know what I am talking about. You want to get promoted, ready and capable. Then someone tells you, 'You Can't.' Do you mean "You don't want me to?", "It's not the right time." "It's not the right time for you to groom someone for a leadership role"? Or some other answer? In a 1:1 to discuss my desires to lead a team, I was told that the manager wasn't going to leave. They liked their job and didn't aspire to be in the next role which, if promoted, would create a vacancy. I would have to leave to get a role like that because there were no roles presently or futuristically. Yet, a role was created for someone else. Are your eyes rolling? Yep. You heard right. What can better serve someone is answering with deliberate and intentional ways to support them. How about the following?

1. I would welcome the opportunity to discuss the position with you.

2. How can I help you move forward?

3. I'd like to put some time on the calendar to discuss your options forward.

4. I would like to help you gain more experience to assist you in honing additional skills, so that when a position presents itself, you are top of mind.

5. Let me reach out to someone who I think can give additional support.

6. Are you able to relocate in the event I am here long term?

Building a bench to create future leaders is good business, really smart business. One never knows what happens among the ranks of leadership. With so much volatility and uncertainty that can take place in an organization, anything can happen at the top. I have seen this occur a number of times and watched the trickle down of leaders hurt an organization's culture and productivity. Sports teams have benches for trained players to step in for other players when needed. The same applies in business. Train your future leaders, continuously.

This type of conversation needs your time and support to guide a person to determine how right they are for a current position. Indeed, are they right for a position at all? It also provides encouragement to either move towards a new position or towards something else that may fit their experiences and passions better. What doesn't work is 'You Can't.'

How did I work through this scenario when it happened to me?

I*Initiated a conversation to set the stage for a candid discussion about my interest in the position to seek feedback and gauge desirability for the manager to support my candidacy.

N*Needed to learn where any hiccups existed, and how to remove any barriers (theirs and mine) to applying for and securing the position.

V*Valued me by engaging with people who could help me and less with those whose behaviors were a hindrance.

E*Engaged and immersed in additional courses to leverage my skill set and build additional competencies.

S*Shared my experience with others to sow seeds of support and provide feedback when needed. Created a "sphere of influence".

T*Trusted my gut for clarity and discernment on whether this was the right time for me and my family.

If you are a manager or team member, before you address anyone: ***STOP*** before you say anything, ***THINK*** and ask questions.

Be **thoughtful**.

'You Can't' can be said in so many ways. Try inserting yourself in someone else's shoes and be cautious with your words. Words matter. 'You cannot do it currently due to these reasons. However, let's work together to get you into tip-top ready shape to be prepared for the next position. This is how I can help you.' Doesn't that sound better?

Be **helpful**.

Helping others is one of the most important traits of a leader. It is not about you. It is about the people whom you are chosen to lead. Lending a hand to support your team will uplift morale and guide your team to do the unthinkable, both professionally and personally.

Focus on being **intentional**.

The mere definition of intention means to be purposeful. It helps to foster a mindset that is positive and supportive. By being intentional, you show others that you care. Empathy is one of the most adored traits in a leader. To feel cared for inspires one to soar even when situations make you want to do otherwise. When you are intentional, your word choices are intentional when conversing.

Be **nurturing**.

To nurture your team means to bring about growth and empowerment. Meeting people where they are, and getting them to where they want or need to be, is what constitutes a paradigm shift. Great leaders adjust their sights on building trust and connection while being vulnerable themselves. Be the leader who people will go to great lengths to support, cheer on, collaborate with, and stay to work with.

<u>Kindness</u> <u>is important</u>.

It's like being in the sand box when you were a kid. The nicer you were, the more kids would come to help you build the sandcastle. Mean kids didn't get support in the sand box. Yes, they were the ones who destroyed the artistry. It was the kind ones who came to help you rebuild. Be that kid.

In the next chapter, we will look at the 4th saying that drives me and many others batty. Guess what it is? Turn the page and let's explore it and learn how to change it. 'It Is What It Is'. Oh my word.

Chapter 5
It Is What It Is

It is what it is, it is what you make it.

—James Durbin

Have you ever heard one of your manager's replies to your inquiry about something and end a statement with 'It Is What It Is'? Did they tell me to let it be? Did they imply that nothing could be done about what I asked? Did they say in a nutshell, 'Deal with whatever has occurred?' Did they really say that nothing could be done and things could not be changed? Because that is exactly what I heard. It is so frustrating to hear it. Ugh.

Okay, maybe the saying works if you are playing a sport like soccer. I happen to know a little something about sitting on the sidelines watching what goes on, on the pitch. The score ends up being 1-0 at the conclusion of the game. The coach replies to a parent who is complaining about the score and how their kid didn't play. The coach says, 'It Is What It Is,' meaning the score is 1-0. No matter the amount of complaining, the score remains the same and their player didn't play. Nothing can be done. The score is the score. When it comes to the player not playing, the coach didn't bring the player in for a reason unbeknownst to the parent.

When you hear 'It Is What It Is' from a manager about something that frustrates you or you find difficult, it can sometimes appear as if they are not looking to devise a solution to the challenge. I have seen and heard this happen several times in teams. I find it disheartening and unlikely to bring collaboration towards changing the outcome of a statement or project.

Change can come at any time. Because 'It Is What It Is' does not mean that it cannot be changed. What it means when confronted in the workplace is that it is going to take extra time and effort to do things differently, and it may not get done due to the bureaucracy that can exist in organizations. Frankly speaking, what is occurring could possibly be happening, but it shouldn't be taken for granted that it doesn't matter to people. There are many managers who are not agile and adept to handle situations without training or leaders to emulate. There are people who exemplify special leadership characteristics that make them natural leaders. One trait that comes to mind in my experiences and those of others is self-awareness. A strong and keen self-awareness can allow even the not so natural leader a window into how to lead in unquestionable times. They see when they need to have a conversation to bridge communication gaps. It is what makes introverts comfortable when someone can see that they are remaining slightly aloof in having a conversation. It is what makes them communicate better and their word choices are intentional and purposeful.

It is extremely helpful for leadership training to include communication and conversational situations to aid in the articulation of what needs to be said instead of the proverbial 'It Is What It Is.' Not everything can be changed at once but, when it is warranted, trying to embody change is an inclusive practice that fuels growth and connectivity. One of the teams that I was a part of experienced the first downsizing of the year. Several 'It Is What It Is' statements circulated among those who were not only displaced from their roles but also those who remained intact in their role. What didn't sit well with me was the response of 'It Is What It Is' as an answer. It was very hard to watch as top-performing employees were grappling to understand why they were downsized and those not performing as well were 'kept.' What would have been helpful would have been a more reasonable explanation as to why. Asking deeper questions by the employee could have provided more answers, but maybe not. But also communicating with intention, how decisions were made, instead of learning later, would have been helpful. While it may be the scenario, it doesn't mean that it isn't relevant to those who are experiencing it. Perhaps a better statement should be the excellent quote by James Durbin at the start of the chapter: 'It is what it is, it is what you make it.' You could see the glass half-full or totally empty. The downsizing could be seen to re-evaluate one's path, should you stay or leave. Either way, it affords a unique opportunity to 'stop, look, and listen' to your gut, and to learn from the process. I and others have found some of the greatest lessons learned when we lost our jobs due to downsizing. The best lesson was persevering in uncertain times and making time to sit still and reflect. I found a silver lining each time something of this nature happened. It also helped to ask questions to understand what was happening on the other side.

How does the statement, 'It is what it is, it is what you make it' resonate with you?

Here's another way to look at it. In some industries, salespeople and their management look at data all day long to gauge the impact of marketing practices, sales interactions, advertisements, and other tactics that guide the decisions of brand partners. Those numbers are sometimes incorrect and do not tell the whole story of a territory and its performance, let alone the quality of the impact made to benefit the customer. On many occasions, those numbers can be challenged. Compensation is paid out according to the incentive plans. Those plans need to change to reflect what is impacting the data points (i.e., data integrity, etc.). Oftentimes, other channels are not included in the compensation. Here's what happens. The sales representative spends a great deal of time becoming the subject matter expert on the product. They meet with all the professionals for whom it is intended to discuss its merits. The product is carried through a channel where the data is not compiled by internal stakeholders or inaccurately credited due to old systems and old ways of thinking. Hence, the representative is not credited for their sale. While the company is rewarded for moving the numbers, the representative isn't. When faced with questions on the outcomes, teams have been met with 'It Is What It Is.' Yikes!

What would it take to go back to the drawing board to bring in experts who understand and have had those experiences, as well as listening to those who don't have the expertise to gain feedback? How could organizations thoroughly examine their antiquated systems to devise current algorithms to tackle 21st century problems? 'It Is What It Is' is not an answer: it's a refusal to adjust and expand possibilities. It reflects an unwillingness to expand one's mind when one is being asked to go the extra mile to affect business outcomes, shift paradigms, change narratives, and grow mindsets. What we ultimately do is continue to operate in a state of flux, old ways of working, too afraid to ask questions, for fear of getting shot down or not heard. It doesn't allow for someone to work in a state of authenticity and fairness. Whether it changes or not isn't what matters. What matters is that it is what you make it: Good or bad. This can begin to stifle creativity and innovation while eradicating trust. This is where deliberate words and diversity of thought and experience come into play.

How did others work through this scenario when it occurred?

I*It Is What It Is until it isn't. They tried not to buy into what could not be changed, while focusing on what could be and how it affected the situation by introducing a new process to help support the business and grow revenue.

N*Navigated through the details to find ways to look at things via different lenses, while gauging perspectives from past successes.

V*Voiced where the changes could improve, while uplifting morale and improving value proposition.

E*Engaged others who understood the problem to identify ways to change.

S*Showed them what "different" looked like by providing feedback and giving ideas.

T*Taught others to look at the data to fuel their understanding to pick up nuances and errors, and to ask questions when the data didn't look right.

When you 'Invest In You,' you are focusing on what you can do to improve outcomes and how your positive feedback and different ways of working can get you to another place. It often takes many eyes to look at a picture yet see the same things in a totally different way. That's the beauty of diversity of thought, mind, and experiential learning.

If you are a manager or team member; before you address anyone: ***STOP*** before you say anything, ***THINK*** and ask questions.

Be **thorough**.

As you think through the various ways in which you can implement changes to improve, gather all available feedback to assist in making informed decisions. Conduct testing to save time and money to assess improvements. Testing helps to remove any bugs before going live.

Honesty is always best.

If you don't know the answer to a question, say so. It is better to say you do not know than to make stuff up and look like an idiot later when you are wrong. No one knows all the answers. The best leaders say they don't know, admit when they are wrong, and find ways to improve. 360 feedback is a gift that's golden if it's given in the right spirit and used to bring value. My coach says. 'It sometimes is not based on a collective perspective, but a one-off incident. This can skew the feedback and cause bias to surface, thus making it a gift you want to put in the trash.'

Be **inquisitive**.

Do better, be better. Surround yourself with mentors and peers where you can ask questions in a safe space. Read the *Harvard Business Review's The Surprising Power of Questions.* Take Dave Crenshaw's LinkedIn course on *The Power of Questions,* which examines how questions can unlock the power to help others grow with Alison Wood Brooks and Leslie K. John.

Navigate all the angles.

Look for ways to bring value as a leader. Managing tasks is easy; leading is hard. Listening helps. Pay for the service of a coach. This is your opportunity to show your agility and willingness to look at a problem in a different kind of way. This is diversity of thought in a nutshell.

<u>Keep it simple</u>.

Humans are simple creatures. No one wants to be bogged down with heavy stuff. Keeping it simple, even when complex, will aid people in their understanding. Listen for clues. Listen and learn.

Turn the page for the 5th and last saying that should be pulled from any manager's or leader's vocabulary. It is similar to 'It Is What It Is,' yet different because it truly deals with the development of processes and how they can stifle creativity and productivity. Go ahead, turn the page. I think you will agree.

Chapter 6
This Is How We've Always Done It

Humans are allergic to change. They love to say, we've always done it this way. I try to fight that. That's why I have a clock on my wall that runs counterclockwise.

—Rear Admiral Grace Hopper

When you are trying to introduce an idea or solution to a problem, how many of you have been met with 'This Is How We've Always Done It'? Raise your hand, stomp your feet, roll your eyes, all of that! I want to scratch my nails on a chalkboard like Whoopi Goldberg did in *Sister Act* when her class was talking so loudly and she had to quieten them! Oh, how I love that movie. That scene gets me every time. And every time that I hear that saying outside of the glitz and glamor of a movie setting, I want to scream and say, "Well, how has that worked out for you?" or "It seems as though there are some gaps and I may have a solution. Have you thought about this?"

I CANNOT stand to hear "This Is How We've Always Done It". I asked people in the workplace if this was a saying that annoyed them. It ranked #1. This chapter could be so long that we could start a new book on this very topic.

Now, let's break this saying down into itty-bitty pieces so that we can see how detrimental it is to someone who has an idea. These seven words are pitiful when put together. Maybe next time, think twice before uttering this nonsensical statement.

It's the year 2024. Imagine if there were no technological advances. We would not be driving cars, electric vehicles to say the least. I saw a self-driving Tesla at Home Depot the other day and thought that was wild! I don't know about you but riding horseback through the streets instead of using highly developed highway systems makes me cringe thinking about it. I remember growing up in Atlanta, Georgia, and watching I-285 being constructed. The day it opened we looped the city with teenage excitement to get across town faster than we ever dreamed. Now, it is one of the most traveled highways in the state and folks can get to the other side of the city in minutes. It is also one that, when it gets backed up, I wish I was on a horse and could gallop on the sides of the highway to my destination! But truly glad, the new highway was constructed.

Think about this. There would be more plagues due to no vaccines. We witnessed what that was like a few years ago with the COVID-19 global pandemic. I am all in for a vaccine and medicines to save lives. I have spent the bulk of my career in the health care arena and still marvel at the discoveries that have been made, launched some of the best pharmaceuticals, and excited for what is on the horizon to help those who need life changing medicines. I would also be typing on a typewriter to create this book instead of a laptop, going back and forth with an encyclopedia or a microfilm to research data. I can access a data bank quickly now. You know, they still make and sell typewriters, but I prefer the computer. What if Steve Jobs was told 'This Is How We've Always Done It'? It was probably why the computer was created. He and his partner, Tim Cook probably said, 'How has that been working for you?' Now, we have Apple.

With my authors' platform, I can link up with some amazing talent across the country to help bring this book to fruition. Let's not forget Facebook, Instagram, X (formerly Twitter), TikTok (not me, but others love it), and LinkedIn. We can keep up with so many people in the blink of an eye and learn things that we never thought we'd care about. Sometimes good and other times, not so good. Nevertheless, it is a different way of communicating and learning. I spent many days of my youth tied to our landline being interrupted by party lines. Remember those? Thank goodness for the iPhone. I can bank with one hand. Flying across the country and world to beautiful places is so fun! Traveling would take forever to get to my favorite spots if we didn't have airplanes. Ah, technological advances sometimes have their drawbacks but, for the most part, they have been welcomed with open arms and I am snapping, swiping, and clapping with glee!

Lastly, I would not be a mother to my beautiful daughter. I am so grateful to the medical community for their advances in fertility health. I will be forever indebted to the science of in-vitro fertilization (IVF). Technology and innovation lead us to opening our eyes to the possibilities of doing something different to conceive. At the time of writing this book, there is an attack on the IVF process for many families who cannot conceive in the traditional way. My voice will be heard on this —no tempering this one!

THIS refers to what you are trying to change, rework, get rid of. It signifies that the thing that drives you crazy is someone's idea that no one wants to change. Maybe, folks think it's too much to change, or maybe they have been so comfortable it can be done in their sleep. I don't know why in the world you would want to interrupt your sleep doing something mundane. Good sleep is good for the body.

IS means present. Now. Today. It refers to the action of being, which is a present tense verb (see *Merriam-Webster*). It is raining. Right now, it is raining. It is time to go to work. The time is here to go to work. It is time to eat dinner. See the pattern? It's present.

HOW says that the way we've done it is this same way. You mean to tell me that for the past several months, years, decades, etc. this has been going on in the same manner? Perhaps with iterations and slight revisions, but for the most part, day in and day out of time, the same thing has been done over and repeatedly? OMG! Who wants to be that comfortable? Isn't life supposed to be full of learning and growing? Why on earth would you want to do something the same way all the time? I change up how I tie my shoes to keep things different and use my left hand more. Sometimes I sleep on the right side of the bed, eat with my left hand, to switch things up a bit.

What have you changed in the past few days?

'How' also means the way in which we do this. How things get done. The manner in how something is prepared, handled, or discussed. 'How' opens a window for discovering different ways of following through on processes. Many organizations are so bogged down with needless processes that it is hard to cut through the minutiae to get anything done. And don't let the process be so archaic that it doesn't even resonate with the present. Check out three processes below to give you an idea of what I am illustrating. See how different they are, while still accomplishing the same outcome? It speaks to the ability to change things up to reflect how you want to move and what you need to do to get there.

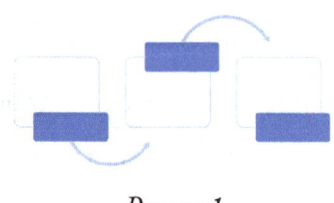

Process 1

Process 2

Process 3

What is bizarre to me is that many people are not bold and courageous enough to challenge the status quo. Because things have been done the same way doesn't mean it's efficient. Approaching processes differently incorporates the diversity of thought to accomplish a task more efficiently—like saving time. I am writing a book on a computer, not handwriting it, thereby saving valuable time to enjoy the beautiful day outside or whatever I want to do further to bring me joy.

We've. We have is ALL of us in a group, company, team, or space. What this is saying is those of us who make the rules around here do it the same way because "We" don't want to change it. It may take "Us" out of our comfort zones. "We" don't want to be told what to do. It is okay that you don't know all the answers. The best leaders surround themselves with people whom they can rely on and may be more experienced than they are. That way, everyone learns. "We" are a collective. A bunch of I's thrown together to make a "We". My leadership coach, Lyn, says 'I isolates us, whereas We weaves us together.' Look at Diagram A below that shows how when we are siloed and focused on I or me, we are far from coming together as a "We".

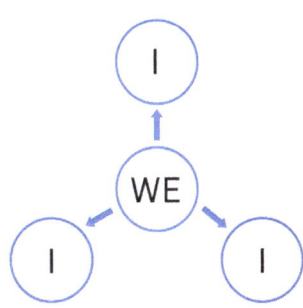

Diagram A

As we focus on listening intently to other points of view and perspectives, we should give ourselves permission to move closer to being centric than being on the outskirts of completing a project that doesn't benefit everyone. Most importantly, streamlining ideas and minimizing errors to overcome obstacles is a win-win.

Always. Always means always. Never changing. The definition of always is regularly, habitually, invariably, customarily, consistently, constantly, perpetually, unceasingly. This basically means ALL THE TIME. When we say, 'This Is How We've Always Done It,' we signal that we are not growing and learning. Diversity of thought means to hear and see other ways of thinking via various experiences. Because we've always done it a certain way does not mean it cannot be done differently. Who says the way we've always done it is better than a way you haven't tried before? If you haven't tried something different, it is hard to really make the argument that your way is the better way, especially if what you are doing isn't working.

It takes courage to step out of your comfort zone and many people who are struggling to lead have a hard time doing so. Instead, they try to do everything rather than delegate. By bringing other people into the fold, those people have a chance to develop. When that happens, teams get stronger, they perform better, and innovation happens. Creativity isn't stifled: It is championed and celebrated.

Check this out. Many of us can attest to joining a team and, after a while, realize they have been doing things the same way over and over while getting the same results—not better results, the same results or close to it. Here is a common scenario. You become a member of a new team. While engaging with the team, you see that a process isn't working as well as it can. You give feedback based on past learnings from a similar situation you've experienced on a previous team. You were also a key player in smoothing out some of the rough edges and improving the outcomes. It worked well for the team, and you were recognized for bringing in some different ideas to the process. You are immediately told, 'Well, This Is How We've Always Done It.' Boom. Door shut. If you are like me, you ask a few poignant questions as to why not be open to change? It may yield some different results that you may be happy with. Nope. 'This is how we've always done it and we aren't going to change it.' Ugh!

How do you think it made others who agreed with the changes and thought they would be good feel? Also, what did it imply to others who might want to come forward with ideas? Would they be met with the same answer? Undoubtedly, it slowed innovation and stifled the creative process. That is why this chapter is focusing on it. It made me feel that I was 'less than' —that my experiences did not matter. It made others feel that they couldn't speak up to share ideas. It also made people not feel connected to the project. When there is no connection, there is no follow-through to completion. It is what I've been saying all along in this book. Words matter. These seven words matter when combined to make a statement, show that we are not willing to change and want to stay locked inside a box. When we allow ourselves to do something differently, it shows our willingness to express ourselves with intention and purpose. It sparks curiosity, creativity, and allows for meaningful dialogue.

How has this saying, 'This Is How We've Always Done It' affected you on teams or in other areas of your life?

How has this saying propelled you to think differently about how you approach your day-to-day business as a change agent?

How has this saying kept you from giving feedback?

Two of the hallmarks of a great manager and leader are the ability and capacity to learn to adapt to different environments. Adaptability is paramount to the success of building one's leadership skills. It provides a genuine way for one to level up one's abilities to be nimble, agile, and curious. Those three characteristics embody great leadership in which to empower others to begin to look at how to do things differently. Whether one chooses to adapt, oftentimes the situations will force you to do so. You need to be ready to move swiftly to adjust with the times, technology, and talents of those whom you lead. It's called a 'pivot.'

Done. According to *Merriam-Webster*, 'done' is the past participle of 'do,' meaning the past tense. Completed it, finished it, ended it. Is there another way to think of this? Let's look at a chef cooking a steak. You're in a restaurant and order a steak. The server asks you how you would like it prepared. You want it well done. Is there another way to cook the meat? Absolutely. Some people like their meat rare or medium. Whatever you choose is your preference. Do you see how words matter?

When we are speaking of this phrase, we are overlooking that something can be done a different way. Making a change is an opportunity to give something or someone else a chance to share perspectives on the possibilities of doing things differently. It opens our hearts and minds to the likelihood that we can do what we are trying to do in another way. Diversity of thought is a good thing. Why would you want everyone to think the same way, do the same thing? That's boring. Think about an alternative path.

Close your eyes for a moment and think of another way to get to your home. Are there varying paths to get there? Can you go up or down the same street or are there alternative routes to bring you home? The same applies to focusing on outcomes. There are various choices that can be taken to reach an outcome that is desired by all. The key is to be brave and risk allowing other perspectives to be shared and heard. When this is done, people feel included. Whether we go the way or not, being heard is the first step in doing something different. Have you heard people say, 'My way or the highway?' What you are saying as a leader is that your way is right. That might or might not be the case. To say it means that you aren't valuing others' opinions. Let's put 'done' to rest and think of other ways to move mountains. Remember, words matter.

Ask yourself the following questions and use them to spark conversation to alter a process or be open to new ideas.

What are some ways in which we can explore doing this differently?

1. What scares you in changing from this process?

2. What are some ways in which you can see this working differently?

3. How might you challenge yourself to step out of your comfort zone?

It. The thing that we want to do or change. Let's go back to *Merriam-Webster*. The meaning of 'it' as a pronoun is used as a subject or indirect object of a verb usually in reference to a lifeless thing. A project is lifeless. When someone says 'This Is How We've Always Done It,' they are usually referring to a process and how it is followed, finished, or conducted. To positively influence the ability to alter 'It', one must acknowledge that the initiative is not working anymore or needs a shift. Better yet, it could be tweaked based on internal and external factors that could seemingly render it useless, inoperable, or less functionable.

Now that we have examined and broken this saying down into small parts with a somewhat negative slant, let's look at how we can turn it into something positive. This can be done by looking at it from different vantage points. Look around, be curious, and ask questions. When building teams and working with collaborators, this is where the diversity of thought and experiences come into play. There have been times when bringing people into the equation with a different lens can soften the trajectory or speed it up to arrive at the destination, while educating the entire group on the movement. One of my former managers, who happened to be a dynamic leader, said 'Let's go slow to go fast.' It allowed us to look at THIS as a small hill to climb and not a colossal mountain to get under or over. As a team, we were able to reach our goals as we paced ourselves to take small steps instead of large leaps. When the time came for us to navigate rough terrain, we were able to move quickly due to our 'Go slow to go fast' mindset.

Ask questions to foster collaborative conversations to assert where people have had success and failures. Allow people to share their ideas. People want to be heard. Listen. Many of my best lessons come from having failed at something. I love the quote from Nelson Mandela: 'I never lose. Either I win or I learn.' This is my t-shirt and I wear it often because it resonates with me and reminds me that all lessons are valuable teachers in building patience and growth!

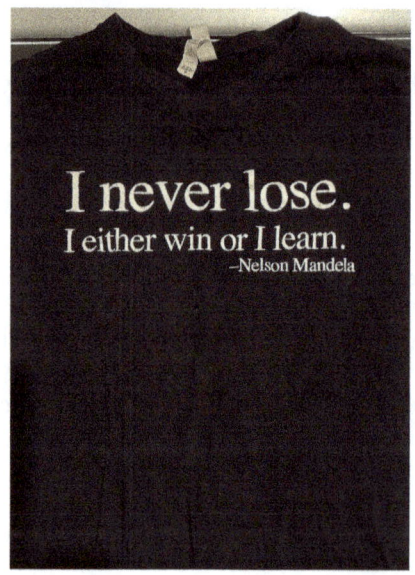

Some great questions to ask are:

1. What one thing did you learn about your last successful project?

2. What would you have done differently to further its success?

3. How would you share your lessons with others?

4. What did you learn about a project that didn't go so well?

Sharing experiential learnings and helping others to engage allows you to lead with encouragement from the seat in which you sit. Mountains become small hills when everyone is invested in the climb. What questions would you ask to get people thinking along this path?

Is. From the meaning outlined earlier, we know that this means "present." As we make suggestions for positive inclusion, let's add in some ideas on how to address this. Some curious questions to present could go like this:

How does this impact how we are doing now?

1. What are some ways for us to alter or revise what was done in the past to make it relevant for the present?

2. Who do we need to bring into the room to help us move from A→B?

3. What are some positives that can come moving from A→B?

See how these slant the conversation to a more positive and collaborative way of gaining information? It helps to open the floor to ideas by asking open-ended questions. It helps to open minds to hearing other ways of thinking. It opens our hearts to perhaps someone in a different light. This is the power of diversity and how inclusion fosters collaboration and ultimately moves the needle on successful outcomes. We have two ears and one mouth for a reason. I can honestly say that I have learned to listen more intently and purposefully to engage better as a leader. Listening helped me to engage in many wonderful conversations with my daughter as she was growing up and developing her wings to fly the nest. I am always learning. I am a consummate sales professional and my inclination is to fix something, offer education, and support. Learning to listen well has helped me to help others in ways that I could not have imagined.

You never know what will become of situations if people don't have an opportunity to weigh in and express whether they have had either similar or different experiences. By looking at situations differently, bringing other people into the mix who otherwise would not be engaged helps to build camaraderie and connection, and to enlist their support. With that, everyone becomes accountable for the success and/or failure of the initiative.

How. We can ask several questions to understand how to move forward with solutions to a problem or obstacle.

1. What have we learned that can help us move forward?

2. How did we address obstacles that arose?

3. How did we improve the outcomes despite full buy-in?

What additional questions can you think of to help you assess a situation going forward?

We've. When we ALL come together to bring collective experiences as well as differing ones, we build trust and respect for those that think, look, and act like us as well as those who don't. Diagram B, below, shows how we come together to collaborate and engage. Think about a team of athletes in your favorite sport. One of mine is football. Can the quarterback win the game by himself? No. There are 11 players on the field for each team at any given time. If the offensive team is on the field, the QB (quarterback) is the leader of the team and calls the plays. Each position has a job to do (they are paid handsomely to do their jobs). The two WRs (wide receivers), RT (right tackle), LT (left tackle), RG (right guard), LG (left guard), C (center), two RBs (running backs), and one TE (tight end) comprise the offensive line. They can win games if everyone is doing their part to focus on executing the play and following through on their position. The minute someone either loses ground or the defensive team does their job better, the play is in jeopardy. Go RAMS!

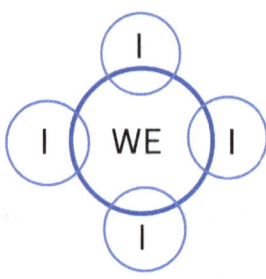

Diagram B

The same applies to any team. It takes more 'We' than 'I' to get the job done. The leader is the one who sets the tone for culture, collaboration, connection, and engagement. If they lack the temperament, skill, and tenets of leadership to foster this type of productive and fun environment, there is no win for the team, the customer, or the company's bottom line. Everyone is accountable. Each person needs to understand how to interact accordingly to move the team forward to positive, desired outcomes.

Who's on your team? Write them here and make a point to engage with them often to build camaraderie, connection, and trust. With trust, teams can move mountains. Without it, they flounder. My team consists of:

1.
2.

3.

4.

5.

What are some ways that you and your team can work together to look at how to change a process for it to work better?

How can you make the team stronger from your vantage point?

How have you been able to convert the 'I' to a 'We' on your team?

What did any push back look like for establishing working as a collective group?

How did I work to engage with others when they say, 'This Is How We've Always Done It'?

I*Initiated conversations to understand why they felt this way and what impacted the decisions. What made it work and what made it not work?

N*Navigated through the process to find ways to look at things from different lenses, while gauging perspectives from past successes.

V*Volunteered to assist in pulling the changes through to completion.

E*Empowered those who believed in the shared vision to serve as champions for change.

S*Shared the vision of what different would look like, and how it could improve processes and make things more efficient.

T*Touched base with naysayers to connect 1:1 to build camaraderie, gather feedback and achieve buy-in for proposed changes.

When you 'Invest In You,' you are actively working to share your vision for success based on documented parameters and addressing concerns. By doing this, you elevate your leadership and show genuine concern for improving processes to satisfy outcomes and improve the bottom line.

If you are a manager or team member; before you address anyone: ***STOP*** before you say anything, ***THINK*** and ask questions.

Be **thoughtful**.

Do not take it personally when someone offers an alternative to making things easier or wanting to simplify processes. This is not about you. It is about simplification and not undergoing mundane tasks that may or may not improve outcomes.

Hear them out.

Listening is a key leadership competency of the best leaders. The ability to hear and ask questions is one of the best traits that a manager can bring to the table. If you're not listening, the chances are you may miss a key component that can shift the narrative and change the outcome of a project.

Be **Imaginative**.

Think outside the box. Sometimes the best laid plans are the simplest and most creative. Throwing things at the wall increases the chance of landing something quite innovative and amazing. Challenge the status quo by bringing ingenuity to the forefront of the conversation. If you have a solution, share it. Your team will appreciate you for standing in the gap for them.

Nurture your inner child.

Have you ever asked a child something and they said, 'No,' without even listening to what you had to say? Don't be that child. Listen. Add the curiosity of your inner child. Children are naturally curious, fearless, and inquisitive. Engage. Ask questions. You will be surprised at what you can learn.

Kindness.

Kindness goes a long way. Don't poo-poo something without understanding it. Acknowledge the fact that someone took the time to examine the process and discuss it with you. Say thank you. Common courtesies are needed today.

'Invest In You' is the way to go in continuing your journey. Trust yourself and put yourself in a position to fulfill your dreams. It's great to have others supporting you along the way, but ultimately you are in the driver's seat. If you receive unwarranted, unsolicited, or negative feedback, make a note of it, be aware of it, and let it go. When we allow ourselves to do something differently, it shows our willingness to express ourselves with intention and purpose. It sparks curiosity, creativity, and allows for meaningful dialogue.

In this next chapter, we will look at some ways to help you get to your destination. Let's 'Invest In You'. You will turn your attention on additional ways to help you. It is important to take charge of your steps towards what you envision for you and those around you.

Chapter 7
Invest In You

Investing in yourself is the best thing you can do. If you've got talents, no one can take them from you.

—Warren Buffet

'Invest In You' always. We've talked about the fact the words matter and how what you say can convey negativity or positivity. If you are intentional in your actions, you will find words to convey your thoughts that lift others and not harm them. Where you make your mistakes, the onus is on you to apologize. We all make mistakes. Your passion is what makes you who you are. Regardless of what anyone says to you, you are not defined by their words or their standards. You were created to be uniquely you, and you matter. Even though someone's reality rules them, it does not have to rule you. It may be what it is like today, but that can change tomorrow. You can be the constant. You can do your best to follow your passions. If the path is rocky, keep on. Sometimes you need to go upwards, sideways, even backwards to get to your destination. The key is getting there. Never, never, never give in or give up on what you believe in.

'Invest In You' sets the course with you being the captain of your ship to reach your destiny. Dig deep down to find out what you want to do and set plans for how to get there.

I*

1. Be intentional on your quest to be the best candidate for whatever you choose to do. Positive affirmations are a must. Find a few favorites and repeat them daily.

2. Introduce yourself to a self-assessment to determine where your strengths lie and how to use your weaknesses as growth components.

3. Identify a leadership coach to work on areas of improvement and how to convey communications in references to sharing accomplishments.

4. Improve skills and work on projects that stretch you. Understand the complexities that exist in your desired areas and grow your expertise in this sector.

N*

1. Have noteworthy conversations with those who can move you along

your path and help you identify alternative positions that build your competencies if needed.

2. Network with your customers to gain a more in-depth awareness of what moves them to do what they do for their constituents and how you can be involved in moving that along.

3. Know who is there for you and keep them close to help guide you.

V*

1. Be visionary in your quest for excellence.

2. Always strive to improve your knowledge and understanding of how you can support others in reaching their goals.

3. Visualize yourself at your destination. Can you see yourself there?

E*

1. Establish a 'village' so that you can have people watch out for you and speak to others about what you want to do. They are your advocates.

2. Having a core group helps to have people around you whom you trust to give you great advice, mentorship, and a safe space in which to reflect and practice.

3. Obtain a certification in your field to keep you learning and engaged.

S*

1. Study great leaders in your sphere to engage and learn from them.

2. Set up monthly 1:1 meetings to connect and establish rapport. Pose questions that spark collaboration and engagement as well as satisfying your curiosity around a certain role or process.

3. Start a journal or use 5 x 7 index cards to keep your notes on for recall. Put your experiences in a SHARE format. Situation, Hindrance, Action Taken, Results Obtained, and Experiential Learnings. This will help you stay concise in your communication of your successes and learnings and help you provide continuity and clarity in your discussions.

T*

1. Trust the process as best you can. Intuition is a powerful motivator. Listen to the small, still inner voice to guide you. Sometimes it is hard, but you will know, based on the environment around you and the people in which you connect. Some people show themselves early, some later, and some not at all. When people show you who they are, believe it. Find others who mesh with your inner beliefs and core to help keep you grounded.

2. Meet people halfway if it feels good to you.

3. Read books and articles that address this issue and put the suggestions to work. I added some books in Chapter 1 that I found helpful. Make your own list and stay intellectually curious.

When you 'Invest In You,' you are moving yourself along a continuum at your own pace. You are defining who you want to be and not who someone else wants you to be. Step into your greatness and never be limited by anyone else's opinions of you. Dream **BIG** and then follow your dreams. The best plans are those that come to us when we are quiet. Find time to be quiet and listen to your heart. Make time to have fun! Never stop learning and always be curious enough to ask one more question. Listen. Talk less.

In the next chapter, we will revisit some important things regarding leaders and managers, so let's rewind.

Chapter 8
Leaders And Managers Rewind

> Management is efficiency in climbing the ladder of success; leadership determines whether the ladder is leaning against the right wall.
>
> —Stephen Covey

If you are a great leader of any group, I want to impress upon you to continue to be great. People choose to work with and stay with leaders who make them feel great about the jobs they do or are doing. I have had some great leaders in my career and have loved learning from them, being guided by them, and, ultimately, being friends with them long after the job has ended. The reason some people never reach the pinnacles of leadership is that they can't get out of their own way to serve anyone other than themselves. It is a self-grandiose movement to be a continual jackass to the people who help make you look great. The words they choose, the actions they take, the lack of action and follow through they exhibit aren't authentic. I honestly don't understand why they can't see it.

What sets great leaders apart is their desire to see the best in people. They choose words that lift and even if they are stern, their words are helpful in grooming one to move forward. Being raised by people who teach you how to relate and include others is important. My parents dared us to treat anyone different because of the color of their skin, even though we were treated differently then and even now because of the color of ours. I can tell you some stories that would make your hair stand on end. I mentioned this in Chapter 1. No matter who you were, what you looked like, what you drove, where you lived, or what school you went to, we were taught to see the best in others despite our differences and celebrate our similarities. True leaders value the gifts brought to the teams that they lead. They trust you to do your job as intended because they hired you and want to feel like they have made a great decision in bringing you on board. They enjoy spending time with you so that they can build a connection with you. Great leaders do things like that. Simon Sinek says, 'Leaders Eat Last.' His book is on the list in Chapter 1.

Whether you consider yourself a leader, manager, or both, your goal is to influence and empower someone to think bigger, do better, be better, dream bigger than what they can imagine. It is moving from A→B with the excitement of making courageous leaps to make it to where you want to be. When the awesome manager was able to recall your kid's name and ask how they were doing, how did that make you feel? Yes, like they cared about you and your family. It is natural for me to ask how you are doing? Everyone wants to have a good day. Who in the world wants to be mad at people every day? That takes too much energy, and you really can't get anything accomplished when you're mad. Being kind and choosing to use words that uplift cost nothing. Be kind.

Leading a group or groups of people calls for us to have a strategic vision. What are we really trying to accomplish here? Where do we need to go, and do we have the right people to get us there? By making the time to assess the inner workings of ideas and plans, and creating a culture of accountability, one can formulate plans to determine if we will get there, intact, and grow in our awareness of what we have accomplished. Self-awareness is key to having an open mind to lead under desirable and not so desirable circumstances. Take a 360-feedback assessment. Do a StrengthsFinder assessment[1] to gauge your strengths and weaknesses. You will gravitate to people who are naturally stronger than you. Learn how to work with those who are different from you.

I suggested it before and have found it extremely helpful to enlist the services of a leadership coach. She has worked wonders to help me see where I am going and how to navigate some of the muddy waters that I have encountered. Being willing to hear the hard things about yourself makes it

---

1. www.gallupstrengthcenter.com

easier to deliver well to others. One time she yelled at me because I wasn't listening. I was very anxious about something that we were discussing. It was one of those silent yells that meant, 'Shut up whining and listen' yells. It was the moment I realized I was way out there on a limb, and she was trying to bring me back. We often laugh at that because it is funny now. It wasn't funny then, but I got through it. In that time, I knew that my ability to lead others was a natural fit for my desires to help people be their best selves and get to where they needed and wanted to go. Leaders, if you have a mindset that focuses on lifting and empowering others, I commend you. If your desires are selfish in nature, it's rude and you won't last long—your people won't follow you.

Managing tasks can be done by anyone, but leading someone is a whole other story. So, managers, don't be exasperated by your inability to manage tasks all day. Leading is hard work; managing is relatively easy. Managing reports and other daily duties is far easier than helping someone determine how to move through their career to best serve others while using their gifts to take care of their families and fulfill their purpose. Help someone navigate a real problem—especially in a world where the stakes are high, with friends pulling in friends, competent or not. Many are not taking the time to get adequately trained on leading with emotional intelligence, using critical thinking skills and empathy. I mentioned the Peter Principle in Chapter 1. It is alive and well everywhere.

Think of this mnemonic to help you remember the importance of leadership no matter whether you are a manager or a leader. You should do this to support others honorably and courageously:

L-learn from others. You'll make mistakes. Your people will make mistakes. Apologize. Allow them to apologize too.

E-empower people to be the best versions of themselves.

A-authenticity matters. If you are yourself, it allows everyone to be transparent about who they are. Be accountable for your actions.

D-develop allies. You cannot do anything alone. It takes a village.

E-empathy goes a long way. Care about your people and someone other than yourself. Connect with your people and stay connected.

R-respect yourself and respect your people. Disrespect is a disease. Don't let it consume you. There aren't Band-Aids® big enough to cover the scars you leave by disrespecting someone.

S-selfless acts bring people to the table. Selfishness means it's about you. It's not. Who likes to eat alone at the table?

H-humor can be a cure for ineptness. Laugh at yourself. Giggle and snort laughter if you want to. If you can learn from your mistakes, that's called winning. Haters are going to hate anyway. Say, 'Bless your heart' in your head. Smile and keep it moving.

I-intelligent attitudes keep learning. Stay curious. Always keep learning and growing.

P-passionate people persevere. It fuels your growth as a leader. Never let it die. It dies with you, yet the legacy of you lives on.

You build it, they will come. Great leaders can bring the most audacious team together to do extraordinary things. It takes trust, collaboration, connection, communication, and respect. Folks follow great leaders—they sure as heck leave a bad manager. Be one of the great ones that they stick to like a gymnast's landing!

As you move towards leading everyone and ensuring people feel valued, 'Inclusive leadership' is key. When you lead with an inclusive mindset, you are more intentional in how you show up and how you expect others to show up as well. Your words will be purposeful. Do you know what that means? Turn the page and see how you can be a dynamic leader, no matter the title or the table you're sitting at!

Chapter 9
Inclusive Leadership

Why is Inclusive Leadership important? Because it is like good cooking: You need a chef (inclusive leader) who knows how to choose good ingredients (diversity) and how to combine them using a good recipe (inclusion).

—Thais Compoint

I absolutely love Thais Compoint's quote. If you are a cook or even tried to follow a recipe to make an awesome dish, then you can appreciate what she says and how it resonates so well with her definition of Inclusive Leadership. I like to cook, and I can't even imagine what some of my dishes would taste like if they didn't have the different ingredients to make them taste so good! I can make an awesome guacamole dip and I can't even think about how it would taste without avocados, jalapeños, cilantro, a little bit of cumin, salt, garlic, and lime. It would not be tasty to me.

There is a lot of buzz around Diversity, Equity, and Inclusion (DEI) strategies as of late. Do we keep them? Do we get rid of them? What is it? Is it made up? What continues to perplex me is that this is something that wasn't started yesterday. DEI isn't a thing. DEI practices have been around long before the George Floyd incident in 2020. When I attended Cornell University's program to obtain my certification in Diversity and Inclusion in 2018, I wanted to ensure that I would be the best leader I could be to the people I would ultimately serve in my different organizations. It still helps me in how I handle small microaggressions that come my way. The people and teams I lead deserve to have a leader who can see them for who they are and connect with them despite any differences. If I am bringing my best authentic self to the table, then my team and those with whom I interact will feel good about doing the same and our conversations will be meaningful, due to word choice and convictions. For those of you who are still unsure of what DEI is, let's explore it for a moment.

As a leader, or if you are striving to lead or want to be lead by a dynamic leader, the ability to include people will guide your intentions to choose the right words and actions to help move people forward to achieve insurmountable objectives. You will be able to engage authentically and share your vulnerability to aid in others' growth as well as your own. You are the chef, the teacher, the leader.

Merriam-Webster defines diversity as:

1: the condition of having or being composed of differing elements: Variety *especially*: the inclusion of different types of people (such as people of different races or cultures) in a group or organization, programs intended to promote *diversity* in schools.

2: an instance of being composed of differing elements or qualities: An instance of being diverse.

3: a diversity of opinion.

In its 2015 study on diversity, Why Diversity Matters, (I suggest you read it when you have some time), McKinsey[1] said that companies with **racial/ethnic diversity are 30%** more likely to break financial industry medians and companies with **gender diversity are 15%** more likely to break financial industry medians. Looking at the key data points examined, it was noted that: **more diverse companies/organizations:**

- **perform better financially;**

- **win top talent;**

- **improve customer orientation;**

- **have greater employee engagement and satisfaction; and**

---

1. https://www.mckinsey.-com/capabilities/people-and-organizational-performance/our-insights/why-diversity-matters?

- **have improved decision making.**

Diversity is the data and it matters. I created this word cloud in 2020 to share with a former team as we were bringing our employee resource group (ERG) together for the first time. We were level-setting the entire company to help us move better together and respect each other. When you have more diversity, you are forever learning and developing to make inclusion work to bring about change and innovation to move to a more equitable playing field for everyone. This is diversity. It's who you are.

The diverse aspects of you are inherent in who you are and the environments in which you navigate. Think about this for a moment. How does this resonate with you? Can you draw a little box in your head with some or all the descriptors? It could look like this.

My Diversity Data

Job Level	Professional
Age	30
Thinking Style	Critical
Sex	Female
Nationality	American

This is a sample of your data.

Now that you have done it for you, do it for a few of your friends, colleagues, or family members. See how different you are? Or, perhaps, how similar you are? When thinking of cooking and looking at your favorite recipe, see how the different ingredients are important to the outcome of the delectable dish? Aww, sweet and yummy.

Now, let's talk about inclusion. As a leader, this is what makes great leaders stand out heads above others. It will be one of the reasons the team will follow you and, if they don't, it will be a reason for them to walk out of the door, seeking to be included and valued elsewhere. *The Cambridge Dictionary* defines inclusion in the workplace as ensuring that EVERYONE (shouting) feels valued and respected as an individual. I will add that, if you are an inclusive leader, you will welcome people—no matter who they are—into your village. They will feel good to be themselves because you are yourself. Your curiosity in wanting to know who they are will open doors to understanding how to engage with others, choosing words wisely to build up and not tear down. You, as an inclusive leader, are there to serve your team, organization, and group, despite their inability to be or think like you. Looking at this a different way, think about this scenario.

You are leading a team and one of your team members feels **EXCLUDED** from the group when everyone gets together. Everyone is on the inside and they are on the outside looking in. They aren't quite comfortable in the group yet. People may have excluded them for reasons unknown to you. Think of kids playing in a sandbox who won't play with other kids outside the sandbox. Have you ever felt like this? What do you do to help this situation along? How do you connect with someone who is outside the group? Your word choices will matter in how you make them feel even slightly comfortable to move closer to the group. Ask yourself these questions:

1. Do you know why they are outside the group?

2. Has something occurred that made them uncomfortable?

3. Think about the kids in the sandbox. Kids ask simple questions to show they are interested. Like what's your favorite color, etc. For adults, sports questions, literary questions, etc. can bring about a great conversation. I like, What is your favorite cuisine?

Let's get back to the cooking and chef analogy. You want to make a vegetable soup and the recipe calls for peas, carrots, and potatoes. Look at the bowl below to see how this works. The peas are in the bowl, the carrots and potatoes are being excluded from the recipe. This is how it feels when people are excluded from a group. They are on the outside looking in.

EXCLUSION

A few things to do:

1. Set ground rules for engagement as the leader of the team. Establish that "We" are a team and no one gets left behind or left out.

2. Bring everyone together via an icebreaker or activity to share things about themselves to build camaraderie. Try the 'Cross The Line Exercise' at the end of the book to learn about the differences and similarities of a team. I've shared this with many teams. We learned

a lot about each other and how to appreciate each person. It also helped in how we engaged with one another around boundaries that were set.

3. If anything starts to go downhill (conversations, meetings, etc.), stop it before it's too late. As the leader, don't be the one who leads the madness. **DO NOT** be the instigator. You are the leader and it starts with you.

SEPARATION occurs when a person or persons are on the outside in a bubble by themselves while everyone else is on the inside. This can stink badly because you're not in the group. A bunch of you are on the outside together. Throughout history, we have seen how this has happened and thereby separated groups of people from mainstream success. I will not go into that as there is so much to be said and it has been written about time and time again. Your word choices will enable someone to feel included even when they are on the outside looking in.

With our recipe, our peas, carrots, and potatoes look like this. The carrots and potatoes are in a small little bowl, sitting on the counter hoping to be included in the recipe with the peas.

SEPARATION

As the inclusive leader you can do the following:

- Pull people into the group by addressing any issues that may exist.

- Have conversations with each group member to hear them out on what is potentially holding them back from connecting.

- Don't allow people on the team to have side groups and conversations that alienate other team members.

- Identify leaders within the groups to mediate and work it out. Bring in a coach to facilitate. Be truthful in your assessment. Don't take sides.

When you have been **INTEGRATED** into the group, you are pulled into the big bubble, yet you are still in your small bubble hanging around and not integrating with others. From this illustration, the peas and carrots are in their small bowl, inside the big bowl. This is not a cool place to be, and the inclusive leader should immediately work to understand how the team is moving through this and rectify it so as not to damage the team or the trust that should be built. Your word choice is important. 'We' is a good start.

INTEGRATION

As the inclusive leader you can do the following:

- Help people understand the importance of working as a team.

- Ask questions to gauge everyone's understanding of being in another person's shoes.

- Find other teams that are working well and engage with them.

INCLUSION is what we are aiming for. The bubble has burst, and everyone is connecting and engaging to make the team flow. There are no sidebars, side groups, side texts or small groups. Everyone is vested in ensuring that the team is working together to achieve its goals. With an inclusive leader, it is easy to join in and be your authentic self. If you don't have a leader like this, either manage up and sideways to help them or move out.

When you are working for an inclusive leader, they are more than likely not going to use mundane words to belittle you or, for that matter, words that could embarrass or hurt you in the presence of others. Inclusive leaders are intentional with their actions because they understand it is not about them: It is about the people they serve. This is the recipe for great leadership and great teams, doing great things for the company and organization. Now, we have an even better recipe for an awesome vegetable soup!

INCLUSION

As the inclusive leader you can do the following:

- Set guidelines/ground rules for inclusive team practices.

- Remind team that you operate as a team, no "I".

- Watch the group for a period of time and assess.

- Continuously assess your team and have your team assess you.

- Your people are individuals and they should be treated as individuals. Even if you're trying to be equitable, being fair is critically important in how you converse, and assign projects.

Equity is the end game. Diversity is the data that matters. Inclusion is how one feels in the environment that one is in. Equity is achieved when everyone has what they need to succeed. People confuse equality with equity. In a cool world, everyone is treated in the exact same way, despite their differences. We can all probably recant stories that we've seen or heard about when it comes to equality. You can't avoid it because it is all around us in our daily lives. The question on my mind is, what are WE doing to make it better? What are YOU doing to make it better? Here's a scenario to illustrate what I mean in the workplace.

Equality happens when everyone in a team is treated equally and fairly during their time at work and in their work environment. It's a culture that many companies strive for and are legally held to a higher standard to enforce. Equity comes into play when we are aware that people come to work daily with needs that are different. It is the accommodation of those needs to aid a person in obtaining equal footing in an environment to do their job. Without equality, there is no equity. We need both equality and equity for teams and organizations to work for everyone. To go even further, think about this. Everyone on a team has a computer to do their job, except one person. They have another apparatus that is not equal. Armed with the bells and whistles that a computer can do, those on the team that have a computer are able to decipher data quickly through various reports, while the one person with the other apparatus cannot. Does that seem fair to you?

As an inclusive leader, curiosity helps to bridge gaps with any person or team that you are chosen to lead. When you are invested in others, you become more aware of how you engage with people. You are more prone to choose your words wisely so as not to harm the people you are trusted to lead. If the situation arises where you need to be stern, there are words to choose that can aid one in moving from A→B. In my experience, those skills are missing from many leaders today. It leads to individuals not being grounded either, which means that teams flounder in mediocrity and don't reach their full potential. They are having a hard time moving through to completion of objectives set, while being influenced by divisive players and managing so many tasks. Take a stand. Find, locate, and invest in a leadership coach. Lean into your own implicit biases. You will become a better leader.

As we move to conclude our time together, let's focus on how we can ultimately bring all this together by conversing with intent. It really boils down to effective 'Communication'. Words matter. Let's go.

Chapter 10
Communication Matters

Communication unto the other person that which you would want him to communicate unto you if your positions were reversed.

—Aaron Goldman

Two monologues do not make a dialogue.

—Jeff Daly

When babies are born, we communicate with our precious gifts through human touch. It is one of the most effective ways of conversing with someone that you care about. By holding them, they know we are protecting them as they burrow into our arms. Speaking to them in loving ways, they hear and can tell from our facial expressions or our voice inflections that we are excited to see them. We often get a glimpse of who they are becoming by their smiles back, or by their frowns if something is bothering them, like a wet diaper! This early dialogue is the beginning of the parent—child relationship and can be seen as the foundation for how our children grow up to be good communicators or not, either in the home, school, or workplace. The ability to converse, and do it effectively, helps to build trust, establish rapport, right wrongs, and spread love across a diverse and global world. It can be what builds a relationship or the thing that tears it down. Your goal and mine should be to be truthful in our communication with others and build camaraderie, while establishing working engagements built on trust and respect.

What is communication and how does it play a role in our lives in the workplace? *Merriam-Webster* defines the noun, communication, as:

1. A process by which information exchanged between individuals through a common system of symbols, signs, or behaviors. An exchange of information.

2. Personal rapport.

3. Information communicated, transmitted, or conveyed.

4. A verbal or written message.

The best teams and relationships work extremely well when communication is valued by all parties involved. As the definition above implies, communication is a two-way street, involving both sides—not dominated by any one side, because every side should have the chance to make their thoughts known so that the other party can understand the position that they are coming from. The art of listening is key as well. Listening to hear and understand, not listening to reply, is important. We know that words matter and it is better to use words that aren't harmful to get your points across.

For a moment though, let's look at the differences between men and women and how we get our points across. When discussing this book and its contents with one of my dearest friends, he reminded me that women and men have differing ways of conversing. I can honestly attest to the fact that there is a difference. He is pragmatic in his thinking, whereas I am an empath and I feel. Sometimes I miss what he is saying, because I am thinking he is going to say things in the way I want him to. He listens very well and sometimes misses what I am saying. Could it be that I am not conveying my thoughts as well as I would hope to, or could it be that he is listening with the intent to give advice? He gives great advice and I have made some good decisions because of it. He expresses things differently. He gets his points across, which I can certainly appreciate. He has earned my respect in how he communicates with me and I with him. We talked about the differing ways some men relate to teams versus how some women relate to teams. He said that men on a sports team slap each other on the butt to get motivated, and use expletives and forceful words to get their messages across—it reinforces that they are all in it together. Yes, I have seen that occur on any given Sunday during football season. Men and women are different in how they communicate. A male leader better not slap anyone in his team on the butt to motivate them, because he will be marched to human resources immediately! And the same goes for women leaders. We probably should not do the same. But, sometimes, folks need a little coaxing to perform. A slap on the butt is not the answer. A grown up dialogue is. It's all in what you say and how you say it.

Have you read the book *Men are from Mars, Women from Venus: The Classic Guide to Understanding the Opposite Sex* by John Gray? It was first published in 1992. What I took from the book was that men and women handle conversations differently. It isn't a bad thing. It's who we are, and what works well is how we understand those differences. It's how we learn to appreciate them, and work within the confines of who we are, that makes working relationships work and ultimately makes teams cohesive so that they perform better. It helps us to understand what is being said and not just implied. Let's explore the five sayings again to uncover how to begin to create a respectful conversation that will ensure that clarity and purpose are aligned.

In Chapter 2, we talked about 'Temper Your Passion' and how telling someone that can easily disrupt the flow between manager and employee. We talked about how the manager, leader, and team member should:

- treat others as they would like to be treated;

- hone their skills as a leader (one can lead from any seat);

- influence their followers by engaging authentically;

- never belittle anyone; and

- know their biases.

If you're a manager, leader, or team member, and you're stuck on what to say to someone, instead of using phrases to belittle or hurt someone, try saying these phrases to empower and lift others.

Instead of 'Temper Your Passion,' say:

1. I see that you are very passionate about this subject. Help me understand what drives you and how I may be able to help you, or assist you in moving your project forward?

2. How did you come to enjoy this work so much?

3. Let's work together to help everyone see how this may be a great fit for our team or organization.

The same applies to the employee who is engaged with the manager. When I was told to 'Temper My Passion,' it would have been helpful for me to have asked a few more questions to gauge whether there was an issue I wasn't aware of. If you recall, what was said to me was, "Not everyone exhibits your level of passion," and I was then asked whether I was angry. Then and there, I decided to shut down. I am suggesting that you ask more questions to come to a better understanding so that you can all be on the same page. It can help others to see you and hear you, and to create a harmonious environment within which everyone can thrive.

Perhaps the manager was stressed or dealing with an issue unbeknownst to me, or a project was looming. I could have asked:

1. What do you mean by 'Temper Your Passion'?

2. How would you suggest I express my excitement about this project?

3. Would you be open to a dialogue as to why this is so important to me?

Chapter 3 discussed 'You Are Just ...' and how, when someone places little value on you, it can interfere with a working relationship or, for that matter, any relationship. We said the manager, leader, team member should:

- be tactful;

- practice humility;

- focus on inspiring;

- be nimble; and

- never stop learning—knowledge is power.

Instead of saying 'You Are Just ...', try these:

1. I am really impressed that you took the initiative to speak up and share your thoughts.

2. How about we work collaboratively to engage in how I can support your movement to the next level? Or help you in sharing your ideas?

3. What can I do to help you move forward in your career?

For the employee who is trying to gain a better understanding of what is being said, try these questions to begin a dialogue:

1. What do you mean by saying, "I am just ...?'

2. Has anyone ever said anything to you that made you feel 'less than' in your career? How did you handle it?

3. What is the best way for you to see some of the things that I am doing to bring value to the company and other areas that I support?

In Chapter 4, we explored 'You Can't' and how the saying can be hard to understand in the context given. There should be clarification around why. It helps for better understanding and setting expectations. Managers, leaders, and team members should:

- be thoughtful;

- be helpful;

- focus on being intentional;

- be nurturing; and

- remember that kindness is important.

'You Can't' does not work. Try saying the following to someone to empower them to work towards a successful outcome:

1. There is a lot to do. What if you could break things down into smaller projects to give you ample time to process things?

2. There are a few ways I see that we can do this. How about we make time to sit down and discuss them?

3. Perhaps we can pull in some other collaborators who may have some suggestions on what may work?

Team members could ask more clarifying questions to help you move through this area of understanding:

1. How has the process worked best?

2. How has the process not worked?

3. What is your biggest pain point in moving through this process?

These questions help to bridge a better understanding and can help others be more open to your providing suggestions to aid them in pulling a project through.

'It Is What It Is' is our Chapter 5 focus. What we established in this chapter was to think through what is unchangeable while also giving credence to what can be done to change something if possible. Remember:

- to be thorough;

- that honesty is always best;

- to be inquisitive;

- to navigate all the angles; and

- to keep it simple.

Instead of 'It Is What It Is', try these:

1. There are a few reasons why it works this way today. Let me share them.

2. This is how it is today, but I am open to hearing suggestions as to how we can shift it tomorrow.

3. Let's look at why it is this way today, examine where any gaps may be and try to find some new ways of working.

For the employee who is sick and tired of hearing this saying, try asking these questions:

1. How has that worked out for all of those involved?

2. Has the process opened new ways of working to bring about the same or different outcomes?

3. What else can we do differently to bring this process/procedure to fruition?

And the one that drives people senseless in Chapter 6: 'This Is How We've Always Done It.' We talked about this antiquated way of thinking in pulling processes through. It is an old saying that should be 'retired' because it's not innovative and is out of touch with reality. Try instead to:

- be thoughtful;
- hear people out;
- be imaginative;
- nurture your inner child; and
- practice kindness.

As an employee and team member, think of the questions below as a way to spark conversation and bring options to the forefront:

1. We have done it this way because no one wants to tackle another way and this is easier. Do you have ideas as to how we can do this?

2. If you are willing to show us another way, let's look at it. We are open to it.

3. What would you suggest we do to rectify the situation?

By listening intently to what is being said, how it is being said, and the purposeful intention of it, we can build better communication and erase the negativity that can surround both our workplace and our personal relationships. When you don't understand what is being conveyed, ask simple questions to help elicit an answer. There is nothing wrong with asking a question for better understanding. What is wrong is sitting there seething because you didn't ask, and now you've tuned out and the person you are conversing with has no idea that there is a disconnect. You may get the answer you need and maybe not. What does work is the intrinsic desire to ensure that everyone's ideas and thoughts are heard.

Robin Williams, who was one of my favorite actors (remember *Mrs. Doubtfire?*) said, 'No matter what people tell you, words and ideas can change the world.' Your authenticity is a gift. Stand in your truth. Even though someone has always done it a certain way, there will be another way to reach a goal or outcome. Step outside the box and do not ever restrict yourself to someone else's limits. You deserve to *have* a great leader. Everyone does. You also can *be* a great leader from your seat, without a title. If you are not able to have a great leader, go prepare and become one. Respect the people you serve. Everyone deserves respect—no matter how different they are from you or, for that matter, how similar.

As you move through life and your career journey, it helps to reflect and understand your purpose for where you are and why you're there. I can tell you from experience that self-reflection is a beautiful thing. We will not always get things right, but the most important thing is that we learn to live with our decisions, our successes, and our failures. They are great teachers of patience and perseverance in the pursuit of making an impact as a leader. Let the following five sayings penetrate your core, don't say them, and use your words to lift others to greater heights, and therefore lifting you alongside them. Don't let someone's negative words penetrate your core and infiltrate your soul. Let's close it out …

Temper Your Passion.

- Never, ever 'Temper Your Passion.' It is what fuels you to be you every single day, 365 days in a year. It is what guides your moral compass to build the life you want for you and perhaps your family.

- Never let the fire be extinguished by anyone. It is what helps you care for others. Be on fire every single day to what matters most.

- Serve others.

- Do and say the right things. Ask questions if the answers are not clear.

- Words matter.

You Are Just.

- You are an awesome human being created to be uniquely you.

- You are special indeed. With preparation and guidance, you can climb mountains. You can reach the mountaintop, maybe not in a single leap, but with a slow, purposeful climb. Listen to Miley Cyrus' song, '*The Climb*'. It is amazing.

- You are not defined by anyone's thoughts of you.

- You are enough. Never settle for being less than your authentic self.

- If you cannot be your authentic self, go somewhere where you can be truthful to who you are.

- You matter.

You Can't.

- You can, not today, but maybe tomorrow. Find a way.

- "Never, never, never give up." We have one life to live. Live it with intention.

- Try and try again. My dad used to tell us that success was failure turned inside out. This came from a poem by John Greenleaf Whittier, which you will find at the end of this book. I had it on my bedroom door for years as a kid. Read it.

- Gain clarity by asking poignant questions for better understanding.

- You can. It may take time, but it will be worth the effort if that is what you are to do.

It Is What It Is.

- It is not and it doesn't have to be if it needs changing.

- Change it. If change didn't occur, we'd be stuck in old ways and old thinking. At least some of us see the value in changing.

- Be curious. If you can see it, do it.

- Challenge the status quo respectfully.

- "Be the change you wish to see in the world"—Gandhi.

- Change is good. Do it.

This Is How We've Always Done It.

- My Mom and Dad used to say, "If it isn't broke, don't fix it." I was of the mind that, if it was broken, I'm fixing it. Share your vision, get consensus. Go for it.

- Never stop engaging and collaborating to share your vision. One day someone will see it and hear it. Perhaps, your team, organization, and the world will be better for it. I'm rooting for you.

- Clarify for understanding and give it all you've got.

- Thank God for the dreamers. Dreams start the fire.

Let's tie this up with a bow and get you on your merry way. You matter. What's next? Turn now ...

Chapter 11
Conclusion

Words matter. Remember you are one of the greatest assets a company has in its arsenal. And yes—we are all replaceable. As soon as you leave, they will replace you. But, while you are there, make a dent. Develop yourself. Develop others. You are valuable the way you are. Let no one's opinion of you interfere with your ability to be great and do great things on behalf of the people you contact and/or the people you serve. Ask "Why Did You Say That?" Listen.

Communication matters and word choice is key to truly engaging in meaningful and purposeful work to make our work and personal environments conducive to reaching goals and outcomes—and, for that matter, relationships to thrive. When employees feel seen and heard, they are more likely to perform better. When they feel supported in their quests for connectivity, they feel included, which helps to build solid teams that trust one another. By deciding to intentionally guide conversations to a full understanding of each party involved, one sets a standard for inclusive partnership and authentic collaboration. These types of interactions afford all parties the opportunity to decide if and how they want to play in the work game. After all, it is a game—one of quick wit skill and determination to think outside the box and be a curious learner, while all the time mastering the art of communication and inclusion. When the mastery of caring for others ranks among the highest in how we communicate and collaborate, only then can we question without judgment and bring about full self-awareness in our dealings with others. That includes senior leaders and those not so senior. It is what Inclusive Leadership means to the company's bottom line.

As we navigate the waters of Inclusive Leadership and hold the people who lead us accountable for bringing good people to lead teams and for building great cultures, I ask you to do a few things to ensure that you feel good where you are and being your best self at work.

First, if you are lacking in any area that you need to adjust or re-adjust in your thinking process, do it. Critical thinking skills are important these days as organizations build in technological advances. Innovation and creativity will catapult company growth. Take a few courses. Read a few good books, see Chapter 1, Leaders and Managers. LinkedIn offers excellent courses to bridge learning gaps and support expanding your knowledge. Get a certification. Project Management, Data
Analytics, Organizational Management, Leadership Agility, Inclusive Leadership, etc. are some good courses to assist you. Take a foreign language. I've used Babbel or Pimsleur to take Spanish, French, and Italian so that you can

communicate with others if needed. Run a non-profit. Sit on a board. Chair a board.

Second, when you 'Invest In You', you will be giving yourself the best chance of landing a great opportunity and hopefully engaging with a great leader while you're becoming one yourself. And remember, it's not about the title: The title gives opportunity, but not all who receive the opportunity care enough to motivate and move others forward. Be the one who cares and lifts others. And, as my Dad said, "Never let anyone rain on your parade."

Thirdly, you can connect with us at the Leadership Language Practice for usable information in this book. Reach out at https://leadershiplanguage practice.com. if you have questions. We are here to support your leadership journey.

Lastly, after you've asked all the right questions, and the answers don't apply to you, where you are isn't feeding your passions and you see no way forward to be the best you can be, walk, skip, run out the door. Close it. Manage the lessons. Take a leap of faith. Heck, build your own table. Have you ever witnessed a squirrel jump from one tree to the next? Be a squirrel. There is no prize for staying in a position or somewhere where you are not valued or seen. What you don't want to happen is for you to be using up some of those 90,000 workplace hours trying to convince someone you are worthy to be treated fairly and that your ideas are valid. If you're left feeling dejected and not getting what you need for you and/or your family, and you are not developing, go and plant yourself somewhere else and bloom. There's a big field out there. Be a tree and leave. And remember, Words Matter. You Matter. Peace and blessings to you.

Acknowledgements

Thank you God for ALL of my blessings and the opportunity to share my gifts. This book is dedicated to my parents, Joe and Ruth Tucker, for teaching me that empathic leadership is the foundation for meeting people where they are and stretching the limits of greatness. They are truly missed, but their teachings live on. To my sister, Sherri Brown, and brother, Mark Tucker, for coloring my world with sibling love, and a childhood that kids dream of. Mark transitioned this life as we know it, during the final stages of this book and I thanked him for sharing his extraordinary life with us. I was blessed by his presence. He was proud of me for writing my first book and I was proud of him for living his life Pura Vida. Mark mattered. To my extended family and friends for their unwavering love and support. Your friendship is a timeless treasure. To my nieces and nephews, carpe diem! Life doesn't wait. Go get it! I will ALWAYS be in your corner. To my mentors, you rock more than you know. For the leaders who drove life into my career and continue to champion my journey, I thank you. To Abe Doncel, who gave me a shot at an opportunity that changed my path. One of the best leaders there ever was—thank you for your tutelage.

The path to leading is not linear, nor is it reflected in a title, but truly in the work one does, whom one empowers, and how one responds to adversity as well as success. The people touched by one's humanity, care, and concern for their well-being are of the utmost importance. Big hugs to Cheryl McGuire, my author partner, for her unwavering support as we wrote our first books together. We met by chance in a masterclass for aspiring authors and I could not have been matched with a better partner. The laughs, the tears, the vulnerability in not knowing what the heck we were doing at first, listening to our coach, our peers, and forging on with heart was a lighthouse to my creativity. Cheryl, I am proud to know you. To everyone who was in that special masterclass, I wish you well as you bring forth your books to share your special talents with the world. We did it! A BIG THANK YOU from the bottom of my heart to my sister, Sherri, my coach Lynette Vaughn, and Eric Haynes who gave their first impressions and helped direct my path then and now. Matt Rudnitsky, thank you for your gift of providing a platform to engage, share, and learn how to put our thoughts down, no matter how crazy. My best girls, you all rock! To Karren Davis, Myra Finn, Tara Jaye Frank, Rob Jackson, Jackie Jones, Richard Leong, Roe Reed, and Cindi Smith. I appreciate your feedback. Many thanks to Anne Abel Smith of Abel

Communications for a diligent and thorough copy-edit delivered on time and to BlesseD'Signs for the beautiful cover!

To every team that I have led, we have risen to great heights because of you and your efforts to be amazing servants. Shout out to my previous boards at Dixie Canyon Elementary School PTA, The Buckley School Parents' Association, and National Alumnae Association of Spelman College-Los Angeles. We learned and leveraged our collective talents and served with heart to do unimaginable things. When there were lemons, we made great lemonade. To the incredible administration team and Board of Trustees at James Jordan Middle School, Reseda, California, Dr. Myranda Marsh, Griselda Lara, Paola Guerrero, and Victor Albores, as well as the staff and students. Thank you for allowing me to serve your community with love, respect, and a lot of cupcakes! We built a California Distinguished school together! Le deseo todo lo mejor. Somos familia para siempre. I wish you all the best. We are family forever.

To my daughter, Safia Smith, for your dedication to excellence and undaunted approach to living life authentically. I am so proud of you! May you truly know that words matter, when they are spoken to you, when you say them, and when you carry them in your day-to-day work and throughout life. You are valuable as you are. Your value is not attributed to anyone's thought of you. You are not bound by what people say but created to stand in your purpose and be valued by God. You will make mistakes. Learn from them and never be defined by them, nor let anyone define you because of them. Apologize. Listen to the feedback that is meant to help you, not harm you. I love you to the moon and back!

Every day since I became your mother, and prior to that, I have fought quietly, and sometimes loudly (not apologizing), to make the world a better place. This book captures the essence of some of the pitfalls of working with folks who will try to "ruffle your feathers" and put you in a box. There is no box that can contain your wonderful spirit. May these words penetrate your heart and help you find your purpose. Live life with grace and grit. Be kind. Stand in your truth and, as your granddaddy would say if he were here, "Never, never, never give up and never let anyone rain on your parade." Remain undaunted.

Don't Quit Poem

When things go wrong as they sometimes will,

When the road you're trudging seems all uphill,

When the funds are low and the debts are high

And you want to smile, but you have to sigh,

When care is pressing you down a bit,

Rest if you must, but don't you quit.

Life is strange with its twist and turns,

As every one of us sometimes learns

And many a failure comes about

When he might have won, had he stuck it out;

Don't give up though the pace seems slow—

You may succeed with another blow.

Success is failure turned inside out—

The silver tint to the clouds of doubt,

And you never can tell just how close you are,

It may be near when it seems so far;

So stick to the fight when you're hardest hit—
It's when things get rough that you mustn't quit.
For all the sad words of tongue or pen
The saddest are these: "It might have been!"

—John Greenleaf Whittier (1807–1892)

Cross The Line Exercise

The purpose of this exercise is to gain an appreciation for how we move and identify in our skin, and how this makes us feel in environments where we work and live. Our diversity is not only in our DNA: It is how we move, what we think about, and what we identify with that makes us feel good in and how we belong. It is more about our similarities than our differences. Inclusive leadership is about creating a safe space that allows us to build trust. Building trust is our compass to achieve "big" things together: It connects us.

Draw a line down the center of the room. Choose a spokesperson to lead the exercise. Everyone will stand on one side of the line and face each other. The leader will read a statement. You will 'Cross The Line' if the statement pertains to you. Once we glean where everyone is, go back to your original spot and we will proceed to the next statement. There is no pressure to cross the line if you don't feel comfortable doing so. Let's explore who we are, so that we can respect one another for who we are. Silence. No judging and have fun!

'Cross The Line' if you …

- are the first in your family to go to college.

- have spent more than one year of your adult life outside of the United States.

- were born outside of the United States.

- have five or more siblings.

- are the oldest of your siblings.

- have waited until the last minute and crammed for an exam.

- are an only child.

- are multiracial.

- speak English as your only language.

- worry about balancing career and family.

- have felt threatened because of your race.

- know someone who has been threatened because of their race.

- have done a good job in supporting friends/family who have felt threatened because of their race, sexual orientation, or nationality.

- have been uncomfortable at some point in this exercise.

- can play an instrument well.

- have been bullied or mistreated by someone.

- live in the same state you grew up in.

- have lived in more than 2 states.

- prefer waffles to pancakes.

- prefer SUVs over cars.

- like to travel.

- have been to more than half of the states in the US.

- still own a VCR.

- think summer is the best season.

- still own an MP3 player.

- think dessert should be served before dinner.

- prefer online shopping.

- watch reality shows.

- are a vegetarian.

- prefer Coca-Cola to Pepsi.

- speak multiple languages.

- like to watch sports, live or on television.

- have lied during this exercise.

Discussion:

- How do you feel right now after participating in this exercise?

- What did you learn from this exercise?

- What surprised you during this exercise?

- What might we draw from this exercise that might help us in our daily interactions with other people—i.e., customers, family, colleagues?

- How did you feel when you didn't cross the line?

About the Author

Bridget Tucker Smith has an award-winning 30+ year career in the biotech/pharmaceutical industry. Prior to that, she enjoyed a stint in the entertainment industry with Turner Broadcasting and Home Box Office, as well as Emory University Hospital, where she was a pulmonary function technologist. She is former President of The Buckley School Parents' Association, and two-term PTA President of the award-winning Dixie Canyon Avenue Charter Elementary School in Sherman Oaks, California, where she was supportive in establishing its charter. Her team worked with parents, educators, and legislators to bridge educational gaps while building a state-of-the-art science lab to focus on STEM activities outside the classroom.

Bridget is past Vice President of the National Alumnae Association of Spelman College, Los Angeles (NAASC-LA) chapter, where she co-founded 100SPELMANLA, an annual fundraiser to encourage Los Angeles alumnae to support scholarships for incoming students from the Los Angeles area. She is past Chair of the Board of Trustees, James Jordan Middle School, a California Distinguished School and 2023 California Charter School of the Year. James Jordan Middle School completed a $14 million new site build during the global COVID pandemic to enhance student learning and academic achievement under her leadership.

Bridget and her daughter, Safia, are co-founders of Guard 4 Sports, which produced the US-patented Guard 4 Sports® Short, designed for the female athlete. Bridget holds a Bachelor of Science Degree in Biology from Spelman College, numerous sales and leadership accolades, and certifications in Diversity & Inclusion, and Leadership Agility from Cornell University. She is an advocate for patients, health equity, STEM education, and continues to be a catalyst for change. She is a proud member of Alpha Kappa Alpha Sorority, Incorporated and remains undaunted in her pursuit of excellence. This is her first book.